The complete book of

GREENHOUSE GARDENING

The complete book of
GREENHOUSE GARDENING

Marshall Cavendish London & New York

Published by Marshall Cavendish Books Limited
58 Old Compton Street London W1 V 5 PA

© Marshall Cavendish Limited 1979

First published 1979

Printed in Great Britain by
Colorgraphic Ltd., Leicester
ISBN 0 85685 089 6

CONTENTS

Choosing a greenhouse

A greenhouse, particularly in cooler climates, is an asset to any garden. It extends the range of plants, vegetables and fruits that can be grown and provides a temporary home for young plants. However, as a greenhouse represents a sizeable capital outlay, before you make your purchase it is worth looking at the basic shapes and types of material first. If you have an established greenhouse, you may want to make modifications to get even better results.

Shape

Although there are large numbers of greenhouses available, there are comparatively few different shapes. These, however, are adequate for the needs of the average gardener. In the amateur range there are five main types: barn or span-roof, Dutch, lean-to, three-quarter span, and combined shed and greenhouse.

In recent years, however, greenhouses of unorthodox shapes have been appearing on the market. Some are decorative, and may enhance the appearance of the garden and be perfectly suitable for growing ornamental plants. However, for the down-to-earth business of growing under glass, you need the maximum use of all available space. A square or rectangular floor area is really the most practical, and will give you more space, so that you can grow more plants. A circular or octagonal greenhouse will not give you so much space as a square one of the same length and width; with a circular plan, the area of the four corners is wasted.

Barn or 'span-roof' greenhouse

This type of greenhouse is one of the most popular as it provides the optimum conditions for growing the widest variety of plants under one roof. Barn greenhouses are free-standing and even-sided. This means that you do not have to stoop when working right up against the green-house sides and also that you can conveniently fit in 'staging' (shelving or benches), either permanent or movable, which both provides extra space for plants and enables you to work without bending your back.

Barn greenhouses are available with glass down to the ground. These are ideal for growing crops or plants, such as tomatoes or chrysanthemums, in beds on the floor as they receive the maximum amount of light. They do, however, lose heat more quickly. An alternative is to choose one with a low brick or wooden wall. A compromise is to choose one which is completely glassed to the ground down one side with a low wall on the other side.

'Dutch light' greenhouse

The disadvantage of a straight-sided greenhouse, such as the barn, is that it offers greater resistance to the sun. A design which is a little different in shape is often attractive and this can certainly be said for the Dutch type of structure which has sides that slope outwards at the base. These greenhouses are also glazed with large sheets of glass and this allows maximum light to enter. Several models are equipped with large sliding doors which permit easy access with a barrow and plants. Some of the latest designs have boarded bases which make them much warmer and more economical to heat. These greenhouses are very strong and the best designs are suitably braced internally. This is so well done that the supporting structures do not interfere with plants or working space inside.

The sloping sides do have one advantage. Glass is not totally transparent to light and for this reason more light will pass through it when the glass offers the least resistance to the sun's rays. This can be achieved by placing the glass panes as near as possible at right angles to the sun's rays. For this reason what is known as the 'Dutch light' shape of greenhouse has become commonly used for producing fruit and vegetables, especially by commercial growers.

The home grower will probably find that it is more convenient not to have too great a slope. The extra light admitted by a sloping-sided greenhouse may influence the earliness of a winter crop by a few weeks, and this may bring a useful financial return when marketing produce. The home grower, however, will have to decide for himself whether the advantage of the greater ease of working with vertical sides is greater than slightly later crops. When the greenhouse is used only for late summer to autumn crops, there is usually no necessity for sloping sides.

Lean-to greenhouse

Lean-to greenhouses, whether they are made from wood or metal, have an important part to play in the garden. They are ideal where there is a suitable wall available, and this is usually a house wall. Only the warmest position should be selected and the greenhouse must not be obstructed or overshadowed in any way. You will quickly appreciate the advantage of a lean-to with the convenience of having to walk a few paces only to be inside the greenhouse. Electrical installations can usually be made more easily and cheaply, and where central heating is being considered for domestic purposes, it will be a relatively simple matter to take a pipe and radiator into the greenhouse during installation.

A lean-to model will produce a very wide range of plants and in many instances a bigger selection of choice plants can be grown, as a lean-to can be made much warmer than a detached greenhouse. If a

Opposite: a small greenhouse, as this barn type, extends the garden's range of crops and decorative plants.

wide type is erected it can be used as an extension of the house and will become a pleasant place in which to relax.

Three-quarter span A mixture of the span-roof and lean-to design, a three-quarter span greenhouse has the advantage of being built against a wall but allowing a considerable amount of light in.

Combined shed and greenhouse

There are two distinct designs available.

One is divided longitudinally with a shed in one half and a greenhouse in the other. The shed and greenhouse are, in fact, in halves and join together to make one full span structure. The other design is more conventional and has the shed and greenhouse units butted together end to end. This latter design provides more working space and is very versatile as different sizes of shed or greenhouse unit can be added.

Circular greenhouses A circular greenhouse has been developed which can be positioned with its door facing in any direction. It is attractive in appearance and has a unique ventilation system. The centre dome of the roof can be opened and centre-pivoted, spring-loaded flaps are arranged all around at ground level. These are operated by simple controls just inside the door.

Doors

Greenhouses are sold with hinged or sliding doors. Sliding doors can be used to give extra ventilation, if desired. However, it is easy for soil and other materials to fill the runner in which the door slides, so that it needs continual clearing out and there may be draughts where it does not fit tightly. If possible, it is wise to choose a doorway wide enough to allow the entry of a wheelbarrow.

Glass or plastic?

Plastics are now too often thought of as a substitute for glass. They are definitely not. Glass and plastics each have properties quite unique to themselves, which can be used to considerable advantage. In some cases plastics are much more efficient and convenient, and in others the use of a plastic as a glass substitute will prove a waste of money and time and lead to much disappointment.

To put these materials to their best use it is important to understand their differences. All the plastics are organic materials and are inherently soft by nature. This means they will not weather so well as hard, inorganic glass. In time the surface of plastics becomes worn down or scratched by wind-blown grit and then possibly ingrained with grime. Long exposure to the weather also often brings about chemical changes in plastics causing further loss of transparency.

Nor do plastics have the remarkable property of trapping solar heat, to the extent that glass has. The reason for this is that glass allows certain rays from the sun to pass through it. When these rays strike a surface behind the glass, they are converted to heat radiation, to which glass is far less transparent. Thus most of the heat produced by radiation remains trapped inside the greenhouse. Consequently a glass greenhouse will become quite warm on a bitterly cold winter's day although there is only a little sun shining. Plastics do share this property to some degree, but not nearly so powerfully. The temperature under plastic structures tends to fluctuate more widely with changes in sunlight. Plastics also do not hold artificial heat so well.

From these two vital differences it follows that glass is your best choice for a permanent greenhouse, which you expect to last at least a lifetime, and also for a greenhouse where a moderate amount of regular warmth is desirable. It is therefore best for all crops of a tender nature, such as indoor tomatoes, cucumbers, sweet peppers, melons, or exotic fruits, also for propagation and usually for out-of-season growing, too.

You must take into account a number of other advantages and disadvantages of glass and plastics to help you decide which to use. Although the transparent plastics may allow more light to pass through them than glass, there is a tendency for water vapour to condense in droplets on their surfaces, instead of forming a clear film of condensation as it does on glass. Light is then

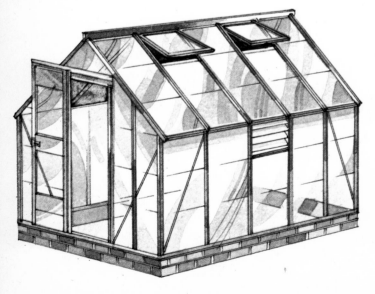

reduced and the constant dripping of water onto crops below may harm them if the plastic is not sloped at the right angle.

Plastic structures are also prone to wind damage, and have even been known to blow away in a gale, so it is essential to see they are well secured. On the other hand, the lighter weight and portability of plastic greenhouses compared to glass are extremely useful features for fruit and vegetable growing. They can be moved about with rotated crops and erected only when needed, leaving the ground free at other times for hardy crops. This way of using plastic is too often overlooked.

Choosing and using plastics

The most extensively used plastic is polythene. It is most important that a special horticultural grade is chosen. This known as UVI (Ultra-violet light Inhibited), and contains substances to prevent the rapid loss of flexibility which ordinary plastics suffer on exposure to sunlight. It should last at least two years without noticeable loss of transparency or strength. This type, of reasonable thickness, is used for do-it-yourself polythene greenhouse kits, which are used by commercial growers as well as home gardeners. The smaller models have a metal or timber (wooden) frame, usually of the conventional barn shape. In the best types, the polythene is 'tailor-made' to slip over the frame. The polythene covers are sold separately so that they can

be easily replaced when needed, without your having to dismantle the frame or buy a new kit. On a larger scale, polythene houses are often tunnel-shaped and the plastic is secured to metal arches. It is possible to buy or make small tunnel-shaped greenhouses, but these have the disadvantage of very limited working space, especially close up to the sides.

Plastics such as PVA and PVC are thicker, longer lasting, and suited to more permanent structures. PVA is quite flexible, so it is sometimes reinforced with wire or nylon. Most of the flexible plastics can be easily cut with scissors and are excellent for making do-it-yourself structures. A very strong and rigid corrugated plastic specially formulated for horticultural use is available, which is claimed to last in perfect condition for at least five years. Other plastics resembling glass in all properties except for hardness have been introduced, but these tend to be expensive.

With the aid of one or other of the plastics it is easy to build a greenhouse yourself, since their lightness and portability, and the ease with which you can cut them to almost any shape, makes the job simple and effortless. Most people find a frame of timber (wood) most convenient. However, be sure to bear in mind that the wood used must never be treated with creosote. This may attack plastics, both staining and weakening them, and the vapours are harmful to plants. Other

wood preservatives should be used cautiously and with reference to the manufacturer's literature.

The great danger with plastic structures is that they can literally 'take off' in a strong wind. It is essential to take special care in anchoring them, and in giving adequate support to large areas of the more flimsy plastics. If it is not possible to carry anchoring materials, such as heavy iron stakes or concrete blocks, to the site of the greenhouse, you can instead use soil to hold down the plastic. For plastics such as polythene it is necessary to allow an excess length of 60cm (2ft) or more where it meets the ground. This excess can then be run down into a trench dug around the perimeter of the greenhouse and buried with soil, which you should tread down firmly afterwards.

Proportion of glass or plastic to framework

A glass-to-ground type of house is nearly always the most generally useful and versatile. If it is fitted with staging, the space below the staging can also be used for crops, since the total glazing will ensure that plenty of light is admitted, low down as well as higher up. However, it will also

Barn or 'span roof' greenhouses (opposite) commonly have aluminium or wooden frames. 'Dutch light' (below left) greenhouses allow good light penetration. A lean-to greenhouse can make an extra room.

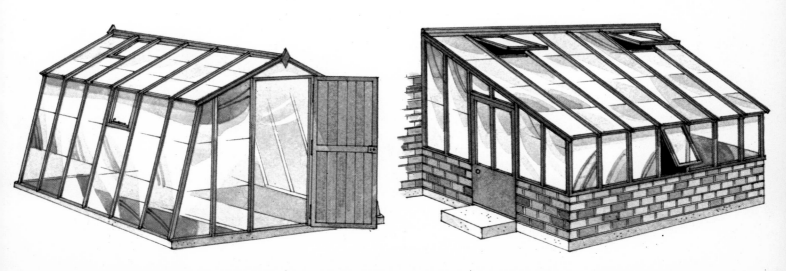

require more artificial heat in the winter. The selection of the site must have a bearing on the type of greenhouse which is purchased. In a very exposed situation it would be wiser to select a model which has the warmer wooden or brick sides.

A base-wall type of greenhouse loses less heat and retains heat better, so that it is preferable for those plants needing warmth and little height. A glass-to-ground house can always be temporarily converted to a base-wall type by fixing panels of an opaque plastic to the lower panes of glass.

A compromise can be made between the all-glass structure and the type with wooden or brick sides. This is a design which has one all-glass front with the other three sides wood or brick to about half way up the sides. Such a design should be sited so that the all-glass front faces south to obtain the maximum benefit from the sun. This model enables you to grow pot plants along one side and crops such as tomatoes or cucumbers in a bed alongside the all-glass front.

Framework

Various materials are used for the greenhouse structure. Wood needs regular upkeep, besides being treated with preservative, in the form of painting or oiling, but it is much more convenient than metal alloys when hooks, supporting wires and

Cheap and less conventional greenhouses are available.

plastic sheeting need to be attached to it. The glazing bars however, being wider than metal ones, cut down the amount of light available to the plants.

Metal alloys, such as aluminium, make for a very well-lit greenhouse and need no upkeep, but the temperature variations can be greater—they can get very hot very quickly. Aluminium greenhouses are relatively expensive, but are becoming increasingly popular because of the other attributes of this metal. It has strength and durability combined with light weight, and, unlike wood, virtually no maintenance, such as treating with preservatives or painting. It is immune to rot, warp, and wood-boring pests, and lends itself to simple forms of glazing avoiding the use of messy permanent putty. Aluminium structures are usually fairly portable and can be taken down and re-erected elsewhere with comparative ease. The narrowness of the glazing bars allows the maximum light to enter the greenhouse. Recently, aluminium frames with white or green plastic coating have been introduced. You may find these more attractive if your greenhouse has to be a conspicuous garden feature.

Concrete is also used; it can make a very heavy-looking structure unless carefully designed, and tends to reduce the light. However, it is extremely long-lasting, needs absolutely no maintenance, and is much more stable.

Plastic walk-in tunnels are cheap

and easy to put up, but do not have a very long life, generally two to four years before the plastic deteriorates and the light transmission becomes poor as a result of the sun shining on the plastic. If you want one of these, get the expected life span of the plastic from the manufacturer before you buy, and get a comparison of the light transmission through various kinds of plastic.

All frameworks, of whatever constructional material, should have adequate braces and struts. Braces where the roof meets the sides are most important on the barn-type shape, to keep the ridge bar from sagging and the sides from bulging.

Size

It is nearly always wise to buy the largest greenhouse you can afford or can fit into the space available. Moreover, for those who wish to specialize in fruit and vegetable growing reasonable room is usually needed to produce a worthwhile amount of crops throughout the year. Many of these crops are hardy, or almost so, and demand little if any artificial heating. This means you do not have to worry about the cost of warming a great area.

A larger greenhouse also has the advantage of a more constant temperature. The volume of air it contains does not gain or lose heat so quickly as does that inside a tiny greenhouse. With less widely fluctuating temperatures, most plants grow better.

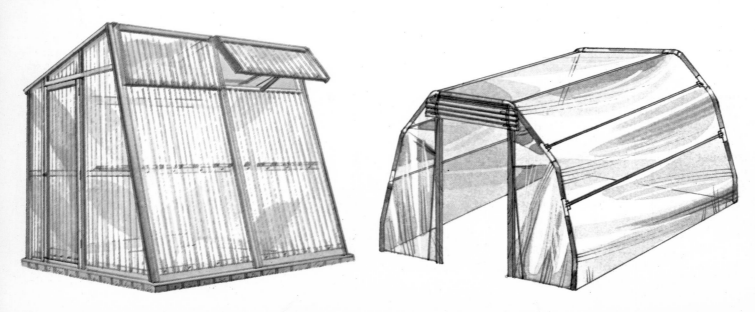

Most modern prefabricated greenhouses, however, do have frames that can be extended at any time. This is a good feature to look for.

However, since lack of room is a frequent problem many gardeners face it is fortunate that manufacturers do offer quite small greenhouses, ranging from 1.9m (6ft 3in) long by 1.37m (4ft 6in) wide. With careful planning even the smallest greenhouse can provide a large variety of produce.

Light

For almost all plants, especially vegetables and fruit, the maximum light is usually vital. All greenhouses should therefore be constructed to admit as much light as possible. Most prefabricated 'erect-yourself' greenhouses bought from shops, stores or direct from the manufacturers are well designed in this respect. If you intend to design and build your own greenhouse, however, avoid using unnecessarily wide or thick glazing bars. Normally, you should not use opaque or coloured glass or plastic. Only perfectly clear colourless kinds are usually suitable, although white is occasionally used.

Ventilation

When selecting a greenhouse, check that it is equipped with plenty of ventilators, or it should be designed so that you can add more if required. With most modern designs it is possible to replace a glass pane with a ventilator; this can be done at any position from floor level to top in the case of glass-to-ground greenhouses. Plastic greenhouses need particularly efficient ventilation, otherwise they are liable to become stuffy and humid very quickly.

There should be at least two in the roof and another in one of the sides. The more there are, the more control you will have over the temperature and humidity. Houses with solid walls often have ventilating grids spaced along the walls below the staging level. If you are going to be away in the daytime, a model with automatic ventilators is well worth considering; besides electrically operated kinds, there are those which

rely on a chemical only.

Beware of confusing ventilation with draughts and always make a critical assessment for faults in constructional design that may lead to draughts. Although ventilation is most important, you must be able to control it yourself. Remember that even a small gap will admit an icy current of air in winter, especially in exposed positions. Sliding doors are, unfortunately, difficult to make draught-proof. Some forms of glazing also allow wide gaps where the panes overlap due to the insertion of metal support strips. Louvred-type vents may also let in much cold air during high winds.

Staging and shelving

When thinking about a greenhouse, most people will want to consider the internal structures as well, particularly staging and shelving or benches.

Staging is very useful for creating extra space on which to put seed trays and plants in pots, for carrying out potting, mixing small amounts of composts, and for other operations. Make sure, however, that the staging does not reduce the light entering the house too much, especially in a lean-to or in a solid-walled house; this should not prove a problem in a glass-to-ground house, where there should be enough light below the staging to grow chrysanthemums or vegetables such as lettuces or other salad crops.

Shelving must allow light to reach all plants and should be firmly supported.

Many manufacturers offer prefabricated staging of lightweight construction, which is easy to erect and take down. Such staging is generally the most useful type because it can be moved around or dismantled to suit the needs of different seasons of the year.

The traditional type of staging is made up of wooden slats on a wooden framework, and this is still very useful. Modern alternatives have metal frameworks supporting wire or plastic netting. The important point with all these is that the holes between the slats or netting allow air and warmth to circulate in winter. To ensure that the house is humid enough in summer, it is a good idea to cover the staging with a sheet of plastic on which you spread a moisture-retaining material, such as peat, grit or vermiculite. Metal trays, filled with gravel or shingle and kept moist, can also be used.

On the other hand, you may need permanent staging, particularly in a heated house used for growing tender plants such as orchids or out-of-season cucumbers. In this case, you can make your own solid and substantial staging from concrete blocks or bricks, which will absorb warmth from the sun during the day and release it at night, with the result that the temperature will fluctuate less. Staging should have a width of at least 60cm (2ft), preferably 90-120cm (3-4ft), and a height of about 90-120cm (3-4ft), so that it is comfortable to work at. If your greenhouse is large enough, it is possible to have staging along the centre as well as along the sides. In a lean-to, staging can be built in tiers so that the plants are all as near the light as possible.

You should never erect any type of staging so that it touches the sides of the greenhouse, otherwise cold air currents may fall to the level of the staging and harm your plants; always leave a gap of 5-7.5cm (2-3in) between the staging and the wall.

Shelving is another useful element in the internal structure, for holding plants in pots, tools and other items. It must be carefully sited so that it does not cast too much shade, and should not be erected too near the glass, or plants may be chilled. If the house is well-designed and not cluttered, there is no need to place plants high up on shelves. It is essential that shelves are firmly and securely supported to bear the considerable weight of pots and moist compost (soil mixture). The manufacturers of many greenhouses can supply shelves and supports specially designed for use in their particular houses.

Do-it-yourself

If you are a handyman, you should be capable of making your own greenhouse, as it is possible to purchase ready-shaped timber (wood) such as glazing bars. Or you could buy one of the many kits available in wood and aluminium, which will enable you to purchase a quality structure more cheaply. The parts are quite easy to assemble and further kits of parts can be purchased later for such important times as staging, extra ventilation, and propagation units. A lean-to version is also available in kit form.

In the case of metal-framed base-walled greenhouses, the frames are designed to rest on a brick wall which should be built to the specifications supplied by the maker of the frame work. It is best to get a professional bricklayer to build it, unless you are confident of making a good job of it yourself. Wooden houses have bases of boards, which are much easier to erect. Sometimes insulating board is used; this is claimed to be as efficient in heat insulation as the thickness of normal brick. Do not use asbestos sheeting because of the dangers which arise from handling this material.

What do you want to grow?

Having read about the different designs of greenhouse available the final, but most important, question to ask yourself is what sort of plants do you wish to grow, and choose a design which is suitable for them. For instance, if you wish to grow mainly tomatoes in the summer and lettuce in the winter you could well choose a greenhouse glazed almost to the ground as both these crops need maximum light and they benefit from the extra glazing. If you are mainly interested in growing pot plants the greenhouse could have partly glazed side walls, the lower half being of wood or brick with staging for the plants level with the side walls. It is also possible to have a greenhouse glazed to the ground on one side and with a low wall on the other side to enable plants to be grown in a border on the glazed side and pot plants on the staging on the other side.

Chrysanthemum growers are particularly concerned with height and, where late-flowering varieties are housed, it is important that there is ample headroom inside the greenhouse. Some manufacturers have been quick to appreciate this need and have introduced special models which have extra height at the eaves for this purpose.

Gardeners wishing to specialize in the cultivation of hardy alpines under glass are catered for by some manufacturers who provide special structures with more ventilators than ordinary greenhouses. Extra items such as special shading and blinds can also be supplied.

Finally, whatever type of greenhouse you buy or build, the infor-

With well-designed shelving and staging it is possible to make maximum use of space and it also allows for an attractive display of decorative plants.

Greenhouses need to be conveniently placed and away from trees.

mation contained in the remaining chapters should enable you to get the maximum amount of use and enjoyment from it.

Selecting a site

Once the greenhouse has been decided upon and ordered, the next step is to select the site. This should be chosen with care so that it is convenient to the house, is in full light and yet sheltered from cold prevailing winds. If it is desired to install water and electricity at the same time or at some future date, the site should be as close to the dwelling house as possible, to keep installation and material costs to a minimum. Also a greenhouse situated far from the house tends to be neglected, especially in bad weather.

The greenhouse must not be situated in a badly drained area or where the ground is so low that water and cold air drains into it.

The best position for a greenhouse is an open one which receives as much sunshine as possible. A lean-to type of greenhouse should always be built facing as near towards south as possible. Not only will this ensure that the greenhouse receives the maximum light, but also that the rear wall will store warmth from the sun during the day and release it at night. This stored warmth is often enough to keep a lean-to house frost-free during the hours of darkness, thereby saving you a good deal of money in heating bills. The heat storage capacity is high with a brick or concrete wall, and you can increase it simply by painting the wall with matt black paint; a black surface absorbs more heat during the day than a pale one, and will release this heat during the night. Free-standing types of greenhouse should be aligned so that they run from north to south.

Although the site should be as open as possible, you may have to make a compromise if you live in a windswept area, particularly if you plan to erect a lightweight plastic greenhouse. Some shelter from prevailing winds, such as a copse of trees, a wall, a fence or a hedge, will help to break their force, but these must not be too near the greenhouse or they will cast shade. Remember that a greenhouse protected from strong winter winds is cheaper to heat.

On no account should you site a greenhouse under trees: as well as casting shade, trees often exude gums which will soil the glass or plastic, while leaves falling on the roof will also reduce the amount of light admitted and prove a nuisance to remove. This warning applies to large trees, especially evergreens. There is no need to avoid a site near small ornamental or fruit trees, provided they are a reasonable distance away.

A position handy for a tap or stand-pipe will save a great deal of walking back and forth with heavy cans of water; during hot weather you will really need a hose, as it will probably be necessary to water all the plants every day, sometimes twice, and to damp down the inside of the house.

The lightness of plastic greenhouses means that they are easy to transport from one site to another; thus they can be erected on a site some distance from your home. They are also less liable than glass to be damaged by vandalism. However, the more flimsy plastics can be slashed with knives, so, if your greenhouse might be left deserted for any considerable time, one of the rigid corrugated plastics is a wise choice, as these are remarkably difficult to damage.

Laying the foundations

Elaborate foundations are now also rarely necessary. Metal-framed structures are usually fitted with 'ground anchors'. The house is erected on firm levelled ground, holes are then dug at intervals around the base, the ground anchors bolted on so that they pass down into the holes, and the holes then filled with a bucket or two of concrete. This avoids the hard and tedious business of handling large quantities of sand and cement.

However, where a more permanent location is desired or necessary the following notes should provide all

Firm foundations are essential for all greenhouses.

the necessary information.

Once the position has been determined, the foundations can be started. The actual dimensions for these are easily checked by the plans most manufacturers can supply before delivery. The type of foundation must depend on the greenhouse. It may be that a low wall has to be built or that, for the sake of extra headroom, slightly higher concrete or brick footings are desired.

Whatever type is required, secure foundations for the concrete or brick walls are essential. When finally erected, a greenhouse, particularly one of the larger models, is very heavy and subsidence will damage glass and joints. To provide the ideal foundations, a trench should be taken out to the limits of the greenhouse sides and ends. This trench should be at least 30cm (1ft) deep and about 20cm (8in) wide. The bottom 20cm (8in) should be lined with rubble. Afterwards, shuttering can be erected to support the concrete until it sets. Where necessary, provision should be made for the entry of water pipes and electric cable. This can be done by inserting short lengths of PVC tubing at the appropriate positions in the foundation.

These can be removed from the set concrete later, thus leaving a suitable hole. If the tubes are of large enough diameter, they can be left in place to provide extra protection for water pipes and cables.

The most suitable concrete mix for foundation work consists of one part of cement, 3¼ parts of sand, 5 parts of shingle; or if mixed ballast is used the proportions should be one part of cement, 6 parts of mixed ballast. As the concrete is placed inside the shuttering, it must be firmed into position with a short length of wood. This prevents the formation of air pockets in the cement which could weaken it. The finished surface of the concrete and shuttering must be about 10-15cm (4-6in) above ground level. Make sure the surface is absolutely level both along its length and across its width. Errors here will result in

gaps under the baseplate and strains in the structure.

The framework should be secured to the concrete and this can be done by the use of Rawlbolts, which are inserted while the concrete is soft. Afterwards, when the concrete is dry, the baseplates can be bored and placed over the threaded heads of the inserted Rawlbolts. The structure is finally secured by tightening nuts on the bolts. A damp-proof course is laid over the concrete before the framework is placed in position.

Unless you are skilled, this work should be done by a bricklayer. It will not take a skilled man long to erect a low brick wall as a base for a greenhouse. An unskilled person will find it very difficult to maintain the necessary accurate level on the brick courses. Breeze blocks are easier to lay but should be faced with cement afterwards.

The erection of a wooden or metal greenhouse is usually a very straightforward affair, provided the assembly instruction sheets are read thoroughly before any work is started. Whenever possible, the assistance of

another person should be sought, especially if a large greenhouse is being assembled. Erection should begin with the plain gable end and one side. When these two units are loosely bolted together, they should stand unsupported. The remaining side sections should be added, followed by the door end. When all four units have been assembled, the roof sections can be carefully slid into position. It may be necessary to make some slight adjustments at this stage until the screw holes in the roof correspond to those in the gable-end roof supports. When the roof has been completed, all the remaining bolts can be tightened. The greenhouse is now ready to be glazed.

Glazing the framework

Few good-quality modern greenhouses require the use of putty for securing the glass panes, and in those that do, a special plastic type that never sets absolutely hard is employed, particularly for metal frames. Some wood-framed greenhouses are made with slotted bars. The glass simply slides easily into

15

these and, surprisingly, they do not leak.

However, for those with greenhouses that do need to be glazed, the process is not complicated. First check the various sizes of glass and appreciate their positions in the structure. There may be only very slight differences in the measurements, but each sheet has its own particular place. Manufacturers state that sufficient putty is supplied. In many instances this is true, but some allow only a small margin for waste. Unless you are very careful, you may find yourself short. It is a good idea to buy in a little extra; it is always useful to have around in case of replacements.

The putty must be worked well before it can be used properly and this means that small amounts must

Puttied glazing helps ensure a draft-free greenhouse. Knead the putty(1) and press it into the rebate (2). Lay the glass on the putty and hold with glazing sprigs (3 & 4). When firm remove excess putty (5 & 6).

be rolled and worked in the hands until they are soft and smooth. The modern system of glazing does not require any putty to be placed on the top edge of the glass when it is in position. All that is necessary is to bed the glass down in a good layer of putty which is run along the rebate of the glazing bars. Too great an economy of putty at this stage will lead to leaks later on. It is very important to clean these rebates before putty is applied to remove dust and any grease or the putty may not stick. A very light application of linseed oil in these rebates will facilitate the even application of putty.

When the glass has been positioned it should be pressed firmly into the putty along its edges. Even pressure should result in surplus putty pushing its way between the glass edges and the glazing bar. When the glass has been secured by tapping in the glazing sprigs, one on each side of the sheet pressing on the surface and one on each bottom edge of the sheet, the surplus putty should be cut off

flush with the surface of the glass. If ample putty rises at the edges of the glass in this way, a waterproof seal should result.

Where Dutch light structures are erected, great care is necessary in handling the large sheets of glass, as they easily shatter while being slid into the grooves in the frame light. When inserting the glass single-handed, stand the light and glass on edge so that there is no 'wobble' or flexing as would occur if the sheet were laid flat. Usually the Dutch light glass is kept in place by nailing small wooden battens along the bottom edge of the glass. These battens are supplied with the lights.

Always keep the glass crate in a dry place, as it is very difficult to extract and separate sheets of wet glass. Wet glass is also difficult to handle and liable to slip between the fingers. Glazing is a task which should never be rushed. Where necessary the structure can be protected from the elements by fastening sheets of plastic to it so that the glazing bars are kept dry and clean.

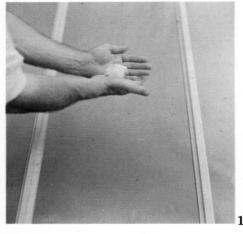

1

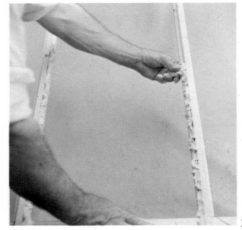

2

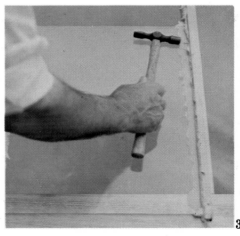

3

4

5

6

Greenhouse management

Greenhouse plants live in a complete, miniature environment or 'climate' which you create and control. The most important factors in the greenhouse environment are air, light, water and heat. You should regulate the amounts of each to suit the particular needs of the plants you are growing, and at the same time take into account the effects of greenhouse growing; some standard equipment — possibly automatic — will greatly help to maintain the right kind of environment for your plants.

Ventilation

Position and choice of ventilators

Roof ventilators should be situated as high as possible, since warm air rises and will escape most easily from the highest point. In houses fitted with staging it is usual to have the side ventilators at staging level, but, for a glass-to-ground house, having them fitted at the bottom of the house will give better air circulation in summer. The warm air, being lighter, will rise to pass out through roof ventilators, drawing fresh, cool air in through the bottom ventilators. In this way the air will be changed frequently and cannot become stale.

Generally, the conventional ventilator with hinges and stay bar is still suitable, although there are also very good modern design with louvred vents; in some cases, however, the latter do not close to give an airtight seal, and may even admit a considerable draught of cold air. It is essential to check this point before buying louvred ventilators.

Automatic ventilation

Automatic equipment is of great help in the greenhouse, since it can do much to regulate different aspects of the greenhouse environment, and

will eliminate worry as to how your plants are faring when you are away.

Electrically controlled ventilators are available, but these are really only suitable for the larger greenhouse. The best choice for the smaller greenhouse is an ingenious device which requires no electricity, and which opens and closes the ventilators according to changes in temperature. This device is especially useful where crops such as tomatoes or cucumbers are being grown, or where, of course, there is no electricity supply. It operates through the expansion and contraction of a special petroleum compound in a cylinder. This movement controls a piston which is connected to a system of levers, which are in turn attached to the ventilator. A very small movement of the piston will consequently open or close quite a large ventilator. You can set it up to operate at any desired temperature.

Undoubtedly extremely efficient, and adaptable to almost any type of greenhouse (including plastic types), is the electric fan. This is designed to

Good ventilation is important for maintaining healthy growing conditions.

blow air out of the greenhouse and is fitted with louvres on the outside so that wind cannot blow in when the fan is off. It is controlled by a special type of thermostat that switches the fan on when the temperature rises above a pre-set point. Control can be very accurate indeed with a good thermostat.

Manufacturers offer a range of fans with different air-moving capacities to suit greenhouses of different sizes. For 500 cubic feet a 23cm (9in) diameter fan is usually adequate For a capacity of up of 28 cu m (1000 cubic feet) a 30cm (12in) fan will be necessary. It is generally best to position the fan high up in the wall furthest from the greenhouse door. It will then draw a current of air through the greenhouse if a ventilator or two is left open at the door end; alternatively, if your greenhouse has a sliding door, you can leave this ajar.

A disadvantage with fan vintilation is that it may tend to cause rapid drying out of the atmosphere. It is most desirable to use it in combination with some form of automatic watering or damping-down.

Shading the greenhouse

During the summer, you should shade greenhouse plants to protect them from scorching in strong sunlight, and to prevent the temperature in the house from rising too high. Your aim should be to provide just enough shading — not too little or too much.

In some cases, you can provide shade by using white polythene (plastic sheeting) in the construction of plastic greenhouses; suitable instances are where you are growing crops liable to be damaged by direct sunshine, and where the greenhouse contains dormant fruit trees or bushes needing winter protection but little or no forcing of early growth.

The more usual methods of protecting greenhouse plants, however, are to use blinds or shading paints. It is extraordinary that green blinds and paints are still commonly used, because the colour green has been clearly demonstrated to be a very poor choice in this respect, as it absorbs heat rather than repels it. There is no doubt that the best colour for shading is white.

If you want to use blinds, remember that the exterior slatted type is the most efficient at keeping the greenhouse cool. If possible, the blinds should be suspended on rails above the greenhouse roof to allow the reflected and absorbed heat to be dissipated into the air; this will ensure that the sun's rays are stopped before they pass through the glass, which will give the maximum cooling effect. When these blinds are not needed, they can simply be rolled up to the ridge. An additional

A fan ventilator, used with automatic watering, as here, saves the gardener time.

advantage of using exterior blinds is often overlooked: they can be used to protect the greenhouse roof from frost at night.

Beware of buying interior blinds; although they are easy to fit, they are usually wrongly coloured green, and have little effect in keeping the temperature down, although they may protect the plants from direct sun-scorch.

Many gardeners are tempted to save money by improvising home-made blinds from plastic sheeting, hessian (burlap) or some other textile. Blinds made from such materials should be semi-transparent, so as to allow some light to reach the plants. The disadvantage of such blinds, however, is that they are likely to be damaged by winds, and are better made of wooden or aluminium slats, or bamboo canes, as these are more wind-resistant.

Shading paints

Most greenhouse owners find it more convenient to use a shading paint than to use blinds. The modern electrostatic shading paint is supplied as a concentrate that can easily be diluted with water to give any degree of shading required. It is white and is easily applied. Its most useful property is that it cannot be washed off, even by the most torrential rain, but when dry the paint can be wiped off with a dry duster.

If you need a shading paint in a hurry, you can make your own by mixing quicklime or fresh hydrated lime with enough water to give it the consistency of milk. A little size added to the solution will help it to adhere to the surface you are going to paint.

Watering

When it comes to watering your greenhouse plants, you should take care in the choice of water supply. Water collected from gutters and stored in tanks or wooden barrels should be used with caution. It too often contains pests, diseases, weed seeds and algae; and under glass can do more harm than good. In any event, it should never be used on sterilized soils or composts if these

are being used for special crops.

The ideal solution is to have a permanent water supply in the greenhouse; unless the house is a long way from the kitchen it is an easy matter to run a pipe in a trench to the greenhouse and attach a permanent tap inside. Use alkathene plastic pipe which will not burst when the temperature drops below freezing point. Before you install the piping, however, check with your local authority.

Where the soil tends to become wet and waterlogged in winter it may be an advantage to fit the greenhouse with gutters, although this is not usually possible with polythene sheeting houses. Gutters will prevent water shed from the roof seeping into the greenhouse soil, and also allow better control over watering and the humidity of the air. Generally in winter, it is better to restrict watering under glass to the minimum necessary for growing plants. This means keeping the soil moist but not wet.

If you do not want to go to the expense of installing an automatic watering system, you can simply use a watering can. Special metal ones are now available for use in the greenhouse; these are very well balanced, and have nozzles designed to produce the right flow of water. Failing this, you will have to resort to an ordinary metal or plastic type. Remember never to leave water inside a plastic can, or algae may form.

In large greenhouses containing crops, the quickest way of watering is to use a hose. This can also be used for applying foliar feeds, which are dissolved in the water. Special attachments are available for using the hose in this way. A concentrated foliar feed is poured into the reservoir of the special hose fitting, and the hose nozzle used to water the plants in the normal way. The spray of water issuing from the nozzle contains a correctly-measured dose of the foliar feed which is automatically diluted by the water.

Automatic watering

Some form of automatic watering is invaluable, but for this to be reliable

Blinds or shading paint give essential protection from scorch in summer.

you need an easily available permanent supply; failing this, the water can be transferred from a natural source by an electric or wind pump, and stored in a tank at the site.

For most vegetable and fruit crops two methods of automatic watering are particularly useful. The first is *trickle irrigation*, which is especially suitable for crops in rows, whether they are grown directly in the soil or in pots and other containers arranged in lines. The water is distributed to the plants through a pipe line fitted with nozzles or outlets at intervals, and preferably designed to deliver the water to the immediate vicinity of each plant. Various methods can be used to send the water through the pipeline automatically, as required.

One of the simplest and cheapest methods uses a small reservoir fitted with a water valve that can be adjusted by hand to drip-fill the reservoir. When the reservoir is full, it siphons the water into the pipeline. By varying the rate of the drip-filling, any desired frequency of watering can be attained.

The second method is *capillary watering*. This is based on the property of water which causes it to move upwards against gravity through porous or finely divided particles.

Originally sand was extensively used as a capillary material, spread on polythene or plastic sheeting on the greenhouse floor or on the staging. Peat is often more convenient, since it can be more easily discarded at the end of the season, preventing the spread of pests or diseases. Peat is also easier to move to the greenhouse.

Special plastic matting is a relatively modern introduction; this can be cut with scissors to fit staging of any shape and size, and is much neater and simpler to manage than peat or sand. It can also be cleaned before re-use if necessary.

For the capillary method, you must grow your plants in bottomless rings or pots with large, uncorked drainage holes so that the compost can come into close contact with the capillary material. Provided the material is kept moist, water will then move automatically upwards into the pot as the plant roots take up moisture. When setting up the system, the compost in the pots must already be moist to start the flow, otherwise the method will not work.

To keep the capillary material moist, various automatic methods can be employed, or you can use the semi-automatic siphon system described for trickle irrigation. Automatic electrical methods include the so-called 'electronic leaf' and the photo-electric sensor. In both cases an electromagnetic water valve starts or stops the water flow. This can be used to supply sprays for overhead irrigation or to trickle-feed lines, as well as to a bed of capillary material.

Electricity is not essential for the capillary methods, however. The layer of peat or sand or capillary matting can be supplied with water from a gutter running along the front of staging; a constant level of water can be maintained in the gutter by means of a small float-valve sold for the purpose. You can dip glass-fibre wicks into the gutter if you use a

Capillary watering (top and bottom) is automatic and therefore useful time-saving equipment. With this method a cistern maintains water level.

sand layer, or you can arrange the capillary matting so that it dips into the gutter.

If you want the system to operate at floor level, you must either raise the capillary material just above the level of the gutter, or rest the gutter in a shallow trench made in the greenhouse floor. The float-valves can be connected either to a tank serving as a water reservoir or directly to the main water supply.

Damping-down

In summer, when the weather is hot and dry, it is essential to keep the greenhouse air humid. This is best done by the process known as 'damping down', which involves spraying the inside walls of the greenhouse, the staging, the floor and the soil in the borders with water, and should be done once, twice or more often each day, depending on the weather: the hotter and drier the atmosphere, the more often you will need to carry out damping-down operations.

Damping-down reduces the drying-out of plants, since the more humid atmosphere produced cuts down their transpiration rate (the rate at which they lose water from their leaves). This means that you have to do less work in giving plants individual attention with respect to watering.

The great majority of plants do not like very high temperatures, which can harm them irrevocably. Ventilation and shading are, of course, important in reducing temperature, but damping-down can also help if it is coupled with ventilation which will cause the water to evaporate. This is because water needs energy to evaporate, and this energy is taken in the form of heat from the surrounding air.

Damping-down is not necessary during cool weather or during winter. Watering should be reduced and water given to the plants only and not splashed onto the floor.

Both plastic-lined glass greenhouses and plastic greenhouses tend to collect droplets of condensation on their inner surfaces, especially in winter. This cuts down considerably the amount of light that enters the house, and an essential daily

chore is to go round tapping the plastic sharply to shake off the droplets.

The best time to do any watering is in the morning. Plants can use water only during daylight hours, when they are making food by the process of photosynthesis. You should avoid watering the plants later in the day, since if you do it too late, the plants and greenhouse will not dry out before night, and the greenhouse will be humid — such conditions favour the development and spread of fungal diseases.

Heating

Although an unheated frame or greenhouse can provide much interest and enjoyment, the addition of some form of heating will not only extend the range of plants which can be grown but will add considerably to the pleasure you can obtain from your greenhouse.

Artificial heating

There are a number of different ways of providing artificial heating in the greenhouse, and consequently it is often a little difficult for the amateur to make an easy selection or

During hot weather, damping-down helps maintain a humid atmosphere.

decision. The three main types of heating are electricity, solid fuel and oil. Each has its own particular merits and drawbacks. The final decision as to the best type to use can be simplified if certain points are carefully considered. The first must be the amount of money which is available, not only for the initial purchase but for the running of the apparatus afterwards. The second consideration is to choose heating equipment with a heat output suited to your size of greenhouse and the temperature minimum you require. The manufacturers of heating equipment will advise you if you send them full details of the size of your greenhouse, materials of construction, lowest outside temperature expected, and the minimum required inside.

Hot-water pipes

Where high temperatures are needed, the time-honoured method of heating by hot-water pipes is still a practical proposition, since these operate more efficiently at higher temperatures. If you choose this method of heating, however, you should bear in mind the cost of the pipes, boiler, installation and fuel, and also the practicalities of keeping the system going, such as the need to stoke the boiler at night, for instance.

Cheap forms of fuel, such as solid fuels, fuel oil, and possibly natural gas, are best for heating hot-water pipes. It may be more economical to use the fuel employed for domestic heating, if possible, since this means cheaper bulk-buying. Electricity is far too expensive for hot-water-pipe heating.

Electrical heating

For low temperatures, however, electricity becomes a very practical proposition, since it can be used without any waste if suitable equipment is installed. It also operates without needing any attention, and without contaminating the greenhouse atmosphere with fumes. It is excellent for plastic structures that often get very humid and coated with condensation in winter when heated by other means.

Before any form of electric heating can be installed it is necessary to bring the supply of electricity to the greenhouse site. This can be costly if the greenhouse is situated some way away from the source of supply. When positioning a new greenhouse it is important to bear this point in mind. There are two ways in which the supply can be brought to the greenhouse: by underground or by overhead cable. The former is the best method as the cable is unobtrusive and safely out of harm's way. Underground cable is specially protected against mechanical and chemical damage. It is expensive and should be installed where it cannot be damaged by garden tools. Usually the cable is buried beneath the lawn or close by a path. In certain districts it may be permissible to take the cable overhead or against a wall, but you must seek the advice of the local authority beforehand.

Fan heaters are the most efficient types of electric heater, in that they blow warmed air to all parts of the greenhouse and have the additional advantage that they can be moved around. During the summer months the heating elements can be switched

Electrical heating is convenient and efficient but expensive to run.

off and the fan used for air circulation only. They should preferably have a separate rod-type thermostat which switches on both fan and heat together. A continuously running fan is wasteful unless the house is very large or lined with polythene to reduce the losses from sides and roof. A fan heater should be placed near the door and at least 0.6m (2 feet) away from the side or other obstructions. If there is the possibility of drips of water from the staging, the heater must be placed away from it. In a small greenhouse this type of heater may take up valuable working room, although it could be placed to one side while work is carried out. It is also necessary to make quite sure that there are no plants in the direct line of the hot air.

Where maximum internal working room is important, tubular electric heating tubes and convector heaters are also efficient, as they are fastened to the sides of the greenhouse. Banks of tubes can be quickly installed to maintain any desired temperature. Usually a hand-operated or preferably a rod-type thermostat should be wired to these heaters to ensure automatic and economic running. Tubes are best distributed around the house — not too near the sides, and not all banked in one position, as is often the case. Convector heaters draw air in at the base, warm it and send it out hot at the top. They take a little longer to heat up

the greenhouse as their warmth is concentrated just around the unit. These heaters should be situated at one end of the house if it is a small one, or towards the centre in the larger ones.

Soil-warming cables

Electric soil-warming cables are a form of heating specially suited to vegetable growing. Some types can be run direct from the mains, while others use a low-voltage transformer for extra safety. The latter is preferable if you carry out much soil cultivation and there would be a risk of the cable being damaged. The cables are run at a depth below the soil or compost. Often this form of heating is far more economical than air heating, which is often unnecessary for the more hardy crops anyway. Cables vary in size and power rating and again, makers should be consulted and given details of requirements before you buy them. The cables can be controlled by a thermostat, but often a 'dosage' method can be used to control heat output, the cables being switched on manually at suitable times. The bulk of the soil will store warmth for long periods and maintain the temperature.

Mobile heaters

For remote greenhouses, which cannot be connected to an electricity supply or have fuel piped to them, mobile heaters which use natural gas or paraffin for fuel will have to be used. Unfortunately, the former may prove to be the most expensive form of heating, and both will contaminate the greenhouse with water vapour if burners without a flue are used. This could mean excessive condensation: the need to open ventilators to compensate for this will, of course, raise heating costs.

Propagators

Small enclosed propagators are useful for germinating vegetable seeds and raising seedlings. Many different models using soil- and air-warming cables are available. Alternatively, you can buy a small portable propagator, heated by electricity or paraffin oil lamps. If you plan to carry out a great deal of propagation, it will prove cheaper to make your own propagator from a glass cold frame fitted with soil-warming cables and a thermostat, or a wooden box fitted with an electric light bulb or bulbs (see PROPAGATION).

Central heating

Since the advent of central heating it has been possible for the gardener to make use of the domestic supply if a lean-to greenhouse is purchased. The greenhouse can be placed against a warm, sunny wall of the house and a radiator or two can be taken into the greenhouse from the domestic supply. It will be necessary to damp down the greenhouse floor frequently if the floor of the greenhouse is concrete. Central heating is a dry type of heating and a humid atmosphere must be provided to ensure a good growing condition for the plants.

Making the most of the sun

All artificial heating costs money, so it is as well to get the most you can from the free warmth of the sun. A glass greenhouse is its own solar-energy trap. The warmth can be stored by building a substantial staging of concrete. In a glass-to-ground house, concrete blocks — preferably painted with matt black paint — can be arranged under the

Soil warming cables allow accurate control of soil temperature.

staging along a south-facing side so that they receive maximum sunlight.

In winter, it is often wise to keep the south-facing side of a greenhouse reasonably uncluttered by plants, so that plenty of sunlight can penetrate and warm the floor. In winter it is also important to keep the glass sparkling clean. This will then admit as much sunlight as possible, and will also reduce heat radiation from the glass.

Heat insulation

If you have an artificially-heated greenhouse, it is an excellent idea to install some kind of heat insulation, to cut fuel bills and ensure warmth. A lining of polythene sheeting has a similar heat-insulating effect to that produced by double-glazing. A properly erected plastic lining can cut fuel bills by at least 40 per cent.

Use very thin, transparent polythene sheeting; this should trap about 1.3–2.5cm (1–½in) of static air between the glass or plastic outer wall and roof of the greenhouse and the lining. Remember that it is the still, trapped air that forms the insulating layer — if the lining is put up so that there are gaps in it here and there, the air will be able to move about in the insulating layer, whose efficiency will be greatly reduced.

Plastic linings are easy to erect in wood-framed houses; simply tack the polythene to the wood framework using drawing-pins (thumbtacks). A metal-framed house presents more of a problem: the easiest solution is to glue pieces of wooden batten firmly onto the metal framework, so that the polythene sheeting can then be pinned to the wood. It is possible to buy suckers for fitting the sheeting to a metal frame. If you have a metal-framed house which has a flange on the inside of the framework, you may find that attaching the sheeting with clothes pegs is satisfactory. The polythene sheeting can be held together at the edges by smearing them with a little glycerine.

In an east-west orientated greenhouse, it may be best to line only the north-facing roof and side. This ensures maximum sunlight and warmth in winter, which is essential for growing most winter crops. In most cases, it is wise to remove the polythene lining for the warmer months, because condensation can be considerable at this time.

Measuring instruments

Apart from the standard equipment available for regulating water, heat, air and light, there are several other devices which will be of help to the greenhouse gardener.

Weathervane
An often forgotten, but useful and cheap extra is a weathervane, which is best fitted where you can see it from the kitchen or living room. You can then see changes in wind direction at a glance, and this will enable you to adjust the ventilator to prevent wind sweeping through the greenhouse.

Thermometer
Sometimes regarded as a gadget – but in fact a vital piece of equipment for any greenhouse – is a maximum-and-minimum thermometer. This has a double scale, with indicators that show the highest and lowest temperatures that have occurred since the thermometer was set. The indicators are usually small pieces of metal moved with a magnet, although more modern designs have press-button setting, the indicators being

moved by gravity. Dial types are also available.

It is particularly important to have a maximum-and-minimum thermometer in heated houses, so that the performance of the heating equipment can be checked and controlled to avoid waste. Buy a good quality instrument; cheap types often have scales that corrode or otherwise deteriorate in the greenhouse atmosphere, so that they soon become impossible to read. Special soil thermometers can also be bought for checking the temperature of compost in propagators and pots.

Hygrometer
A direct-reading hygrometer, which shows at a glance the humidity of the air (the amount of water it contains) will be especially useful to beginners. This knowledge helps in watering, damping-down, and general control of the greenhouse atmosphere. Small-dial hygrometers are quite cheap and very efficient.

Psychrometer
Another worthwhile instrument is

Soil-warming cables with mist propagation give even temperature and a humid atmosphere for cuttings.

the psychrometer, or 'frost predictor', which actually works by measuring humidity. Provided that it is correctly placed and maintained according to the manufacturer's instructions, it will give reliable warning of frost, enabling you to adjust the greenhouse heating, if necessary, before any damage is done to the plants.

Moisture and fertilizer meters
Beginners may also find useful the modern soil-moisture meters and fertilizer-concentration meters, as these take much of the guesswork out of watering and applying fertilizers. Some soil-moisture meters give a 'dry', 'moist', or 'water' indication on a graduated scale. Other mosture meters (and combined fertilizer-concentration-and-moisture meters) indicate the level of moisture and plant food either by means of lights or a sound signal. Both types need a small battery.

Greenhouse hygiene

Cleanliness and constant vigilance in spotting the first signs of attack by pests or diseases are essential for success in greenhouse gardening. Rubbish and odd items such as old and dirty seed trays and pots, or dirty pea-sticks, should never be stored in the greenhouse, because they will harbour such pests as slugs, snails and earwigs, as well as disease. A serious infestation causes problems and may result in the loss of both time and money. You should inspect your greenhouse crops for any signs of pests or diseases as a matter of daily routine, so that they can be controlled immediately and effectively before they have had a chance to become established.

Make a special point of looking under the foliage of your plants for any pests or disease symptoms. Remove pests by hand if possible; otherwise spray really thoroughly with the safest pesticide available. Treat diseases by spraying or fumigation. You can buy fumigants in handy aerosol packs; other fumigants are lit like fireworks. Automatic fumigation apparatus is available, but this may not always eradicate the

A fumigating bomb is a useful way of controlling greenhouse pests.

pest or disease, and there is also the problem of the greenhouse atmosphere frequently containing pesticide chemicals, which may be inhaled.

The greenhouse should be made as air-tight as possible for fumigation; use wet sacking to block up any cracks. You should not fumigate when the temperature is above 21°C (70°F) or when the house is in bright sunshine, or you may damage the plants. The best time to fumigate is in the evening. After fumigating, close the greenhouse for the night, and ventilate it well the following morning. Always follow the manufacturer's instructions very carefully.

Generally, it is possible to grow plants and to obtain reasonable yields of good-quality crops by growing them in the soil of the greenhouse borders, provided that you take the important precaution of sterilizing the soil and using it for one season only. If you cannot do this, it is best to stand pots or other containers of compost (soil mixture) on the borders and grow crops in these. If you want to retain the appearance of a border, you can sink a trough of compost into the ground. If you have a lightweight plastic greenhouse, however, you can use the border soil for one season, then move the greenhouse to a new patch of soil when the first one is exhausted. This would not be possible, though, unless all the sites

received enough light and were away from overhanging trees.

The importance of using sterilized soil cannot be overstressed. Under cover, unsterilized ground soil tends to become what is known as 'soil sick' in quite a short time. This is because waste products from the plants and excess fertilizers cannot be washed out of the soil by rain, as would normally happen outdoors. Also, pests and diseases are able to build up in greenhouse soil because they are not killed by frost, ultra-violet rays from the sun (which are absorbed by glass and, to a lesser extent, by plastics) or natural predators.

Sterilizing greenhouse soil

The simplest method of sterilization suitable for the home grower is to use the chemical formalin. This must be done well in advance of cultivation, because you must allow at least six weeks for the fumes to disappear from the soil and air before you put any plants in the house.

You can buy formalin, which is a clear liquid, from many garden shops or chemists. Dilute it with water to give a 2% solution, or as directed on the label, and use this according to the instructions. You must make the soil moist before you apply the

A steam soil sterilizer is useful for treating small quantities of soil.

formalin solution. Immediately after you have applied it, cover the soil with plastic sheeting to keep in the fumes overnight. You should subsequently keep the house well ventilated.

Composts (soil mixtures)

You can buy commercial brands of seed and potting composts and of peat-based (loamless) compost from garden shops, centres or nurseries, or you can make your own compost. If you require a fair amount of compost or can share it with a friend or neighbour, it is much cheaper to make your own. Remember, however, when making compost for greenhouse use, that you must use sterilized soil or loam.

Potting composts contain fertilizers, but these are soon used up by the plants and will need to be supplemented by liquid feeds. Use either a soluble fertilizer concentrate containing trace elements or buy separate single-nutrient fertilizers and mix them together, in the proportions suggested by the manufacturers.

A special problem with loamless mixtures is that they dry out very easily. This is because the peat acts like a sponge. If a loamless compost (mixture) dries out, it may prove difficult to get it moist again. Nevertheless, when you do water it, you must ensure that it does not become waterlogged. If it does dry out, you should water it twice in one day, to make sure that it is uniformly moist. The best policy is regular and frequent watering.

Growing bags
Plastic 'growing bags' filled, with a peat-based compost, are also very suitable for greenhouse. These are available in various sizes. They should be laid flat on the greenhouse border and holes cut in the top of the bag according to the manufacturer's instructions, so that the plants can be inserted in the compost. If the ground inside the greenhouse is rough, they can be laid on planks. Correct watering is very important with this method of growing; follow the manufacturer's instructions closely.

Ring culture Another alternative is to use the method of growing known as 'ring culture', which is ideally suited to the cultivation of tomatoes (see page 64).

'Growing bags' contain a mixture, generally peat-based, enriched with essential nutrients. They are particularly suitable in small greenhouses.

Plants and houseplants

What can be grown in a greenhouse depends to a great extent on the minimum temperature that can be maintained in the winter.

Unheated greenhouse

A great deal of interest can, however, be had from a greenhouse with no heating equipment. If you are working to a small budget, an arrangement of this sort is a good beginning; heating equipment can be installed later on as you become more experienced and wish to experiment with a wider range of plants.

An attractive display can be had in an unheated greenhouse by growing mainly hardy plants in pots. These will flower a little earlier than those in the open but the flowers will not be spoilt by inclement weather. Other plants that are usually started into growth early in warmth for summer flowering, can also be grown by starting them later when it is warmer outside.

Shrubs

The camellia is often thought to be tender, possibly because the flowers, which appear early in the year, are sometimes damaged by frost. For this reason the protection of a greenhouse is valuable. All the varieties of *Camellia japonica* will grow happily in pots of lime-free soil, but they should not be cosseted as if they were hothouse plants. *Prunus triloba flore pleno* has double pink flowers and is another fine flowering shrub for the cold greenhouse. The yellow-flowered forsythia and rosy-purple *Rhododendron praecox*, lilacs as well as winter-flowering heathers (*Erica carnea*) will all give a bright display. For flowering in the summer *Hydrangea paniculata grandiflora* produces enormous white flower trusses. It is easily grown in pots and the stems should be cut back severely each spring. The 'hortensia' hydrangea will flower earlier than the species mentioned above and really good blue flowers can be had if the soil is treated with a blueing powder.

Bulbs

These can provide a wonderful dis-

Greenhouse protection helps save camellia flowers from frost damage.

play early in the year. The earliest to flower are 'prepared' daffodils in January followed by 'Paper White' narcissi, the dark blue *Iris reticulata* and named varieties of snowdrop. Other small bulbs well worth growing are miniature daffodils, such as *Narcissus cyclamineus*, *N. bulbocodium* and *N. triandrus albus*, winter-flowering crocuses and *Eranthis hyemalis*, the winter aconite with buttercup-yellow flowers.

For flowering in the summer, lilies such as *L. auratum* and *L. speciosum* look superb grown in pots. Gloxinias and tuberous-rooted begonias are popular plants and the tubers of these can be started into growth in early April.

Other flowers for a spring display, which can be purchased or lifted from the open garden in the autumn and potted up for the cold greenhouse, are wallflowers, dicentras, astilbes, forget-me-nots, polyanthus,

lily-of-the-valley and Christmas roses (*Helleborus niger*).

Cool greenhouses

Although great interest can be had from an unheated greenhouse, a much wider range of plants can obviously be had if the greenhouse has a minimum winter temperature of 10°C (50°F). With the aid of artificial heat it is also easier to mantain a good growing atmosphere or climate for the plants.

Shrubs

As in the cold greenhouse, hardy shrubs such as forsythia and *Prunus triloba* can be brought into the greenhouse in winter for flowering much earlier than those in the open. Camellias will thrive, provided the temperature is not allowed to shoot up too high in the day—this causes the flower buds to drop—and hydrangeas in pots can be made to flower early. Indian azaleas are popular florists' pot plants. These can be kept from year to year in a heated greenhouse, provided they are fed regularly. They flower in winter and early spring and can be put outside for the summer. *Acacia dealbata*, or mimosa, with yellow fluffy flowers and a heady scent can be enjoyed in early spring. There are also a great many ornamental climbers that will enjoy the warmth. The passion flowers, the brightly coloured bougainvilleas, the soft blue *Plumbago capensis* and *Lapageria rosea* with rose pink, waxy bells, all flower in summer.

Bulbs

All the popular bulbs such as daffodils, hyacinths and tulips, can be made to flower in the dark days of winter in a heated greenhouse, but after the pots and bowls are removed from the plunge beds they should be given cool conditions at first and gradually acclimatized to warmer conditions.

Hippeastrums, often mistakenly called amaryllis, have large, handsome flowers and the bulbs may be started into growth in February for spring flowering. Freesia corms, started into growth in August, produce their colourful and scented flowers in February and March; they

A little heat greatly extends the range of plants that can be grown.

29

will grow well in a minimum temperature of 4°C (40°F).

Arum lilies are not true bulbs—they have tuberous roots—but in a heated greenhouse they will flower in the spring. An easily grown and handsome bulb is the Scarborough Lily, *Vallota speciosa*. It can be stood outside for the summer and in August it will produce its vermilion trumpet flowers on stout stems. Flowering a little later, nerines have delightful, glistening flowers in pink, red and white; they differ from many bulbs in that they need to be rested and kept dry in the summer.

Begonia and gloxinia tubers may be started into growth in March for flowering in the summer. Achimenes can be treated similarly, grown in pots or in hanging baskets.

Other flowers that will flourish in a greenhouse with a temperature of 10°C (50°F) in winter are perpetual-flowering carnations — they like light and airy conditions and will flower for most of the year; chrysanthemums for autumn and winter flowering; and fuchsias for the summer.

Pot plants that can be raised from seed in spring and early summer for a display in winter and spring are: *Primula obconica*, *P. malacoides* and calceolarias. Some gardeners, unfortunately, are allergic to *P. obconica* and if they handle plants it sets up an unpleasant skin irritation.

Cyclamen can be grown successfully from seed sown in August, to provide plants for flowering 16 months later. The poor man's orchid, schizanthus, is also easily raised from seed in August for flowering the following spring.

Regal pelargoniums are becoming more popular and they are useful for their handsome flowers borne from June onwards; these are best propagated from cuttings taken in late summer.

The main parents of the regals are *P. cucullatum* and *P. betulinum*; which are indigenous to the coastal regions of South Africa. Hybridization started on the species mainly in England, in France and also in central Europe well over a century ago. These plants should be grown under glass or in the house throughout the year in a temperate climate, although they may be grown outdoors in summer in exceptionally protected places. Two lovely cultivars have been produced that will grow well out of doors in all kinds of weather during the summer months. These are 'Hula' and 'Carefree' from America. These two are the results of crossing the cultivars back to the species. 'Hula' and 'Carefree' do not have flower umbels as large as the true regals but have the advantage of being able to stand up to bad conitions out of doors.

Some recommended cultivars are as follows (dominating colours only are mentioned): 'Annie Hawkins', pink; 'Applause', pink and white; 'Aztec', strawberry pink and white; 'Blythwood', purple and mauve; 'Caprice', pink; 'Carisbrooke', rose pink; 'Doris Frith', white; 'Grand Slam', red; Marie Rober', lavender; 'Muriel Hawkins', pink; 'Rapture', apricot; 'Rhodamine', purple and mauve; and the outstanding sport from 'Grand Slam', 'Lavender Grand Slam'.

The flowering season of the regals has been greatly lengthened within the last five years by the introduction of the new cultivars.

Warm greenhouses

To be able to heat a greenhouse to 13°C (55°F) in winter is expensive, as fuel costs continue to rise, but it is rewarding. Many tropical or 'stove' plants can be cultivated in addition to those already mentioned.

Shrubs

Among the shrubby plants with handsome foliage for a warm greenhouse, most of which are rarely seen, codiaeums (crotons) are outstanding. They have leaves of various shades, brightly marked with green, red, yellow and orange. Dracaenas also have attractively coloured leaves and they include *D. godseffiana* with green, white-spotted leaves and *D. fragrans victoriae* with long green and yellow striped leaves.

Regal pelargoniums are handsome free-flowering cool-greenhouse plants.

The poinsettia, *Euphorbia pul-cherrima*, a popular plant at Christmas time with red rosettes of bracts, needs a warm greenhouse to grow well and so does its close relative *E. fulgens*, which has small orange-red flowers on arching stems in winter.

Gardenias, which are prized for their pure white fragrant flowers, do best in a warm greenhouse. Less commonly seen is *Brunfelsia caly-cina*, an evergreen shrub with purple flowers.

Greenhouse climbers

Many of the most beautiful climbers are too tender to be grown out of doors in most temperate climates but are fine plants for greenhouse or conservatories. They may be grown in large pots or other containers, or planted direct in the greenhouse border. In lean-to greenhouses the plants may be grown against the back wall and trained up and over the rafters. In span-roof greenhouses they are either grown at the end of the house opposite to the door or in

the border below the staging and trained up between the staging and the wall and thence up the rafters. Less vigorous climbers may be grown in pots on the staging and provided with some form of support in the way of canes, etc. Several of these greenhouse climbers make good house plants.

There are numerous exotic climbers. The Madasgacar jasmine, *Stephanotis floribunda* has thick leathery leaves and clusters of white scented flowers. There are also several clerodendrums with colourful flowers; *C. thomsonae* has crimson and white flowers and *C. splendens* produces clusters of red flowers.

Bulbs

Begonias, gloxinias, hippeastrums and smithianthas can all be started into growth in January or early February; seed of begonias and gloxinias can also be sown in January. Apart from these popular types, *Eucharis grandiflora* with beautiful, white and fragrant flowers will revel in a warm greenhouse. The tuberose,

Clerodendrum thomsonae *is a vigorous climber in a warm greenhouse.*

Polianthus tuberosa, is another bulbous plant well worth cultivating for its white, fragrant flowers. Caladiums have tuberous roots and they are grown for their handsome foliage. The tubers can be started into growth after resting in the winter.

Other plants that enjoy a warm greenhouse include coleus and *Begonia rex*, both of which have highly ornamental foliage. Winter-flowering begonias, provide a wonderful display of colour in white, pink or red. Saintpaulias, so popular as room plants, do best in a well-heated greenhouse.

Perpetual flowering carnations

A greenhouse devoted to these can give much satisfaction to the amateur. They are grown in pots or on raised beds.

While the plants will withstand quite low temperatures artificial heat is required to keep carnations

flowering during the winter months. In mild areas of southern France and Italy they are grown commercially in the open, with the emphasis on quantity. This is evidence that the plants require plenty of air and when grown under glass a free circulation of air is most important whenever the weather permits. Excessive humidity must be avoided, although during hot summer days the staging and greenhouse floor should be 'damped down' once, or perhaps twice a day, but the atmosphere should not be damp at night. If the pots are stood on a layer of small shingle damping can easily be done with a watering can or a syringe. Spraying the plants used to be the practice as a check to red spider mite, but water spots the blooms and the pest is better controlled by the use of a greenhouse aerosol.

It is of the utmost importance to start with cuttings or plants obtained from disease-free stock. In recent years 'cultured' cuttings have been available commercially and these form an excellent nucleus on which to start a collection. Cuttings may be taken over many months from October to February, and the strongest shoots from about half-way up a stem which has produced blooms

A well-planted greenhouse can be colourful all through the year.

should be chosen. As the propagating period is long this makes it possible to take time in selecting the best cuttings. Cuttings taken in January and February have the advantage of lengthening days. The cutting should bear about four or five pairs of fully developed leaves and should be severed from the parent plant with a sharp knife and not pulled, as this may damage the stem on which it was growing. Insert the cuttings in pots, or in a propagating frame, containing clean sharp silver sand.

32

Make the base of the cutting firm with the dibber (dibble), placing the cuttings about 4cm (1½) apart. Water the cuttings and stand them in a frame with gentle bottom heat 13-16°C (55°-60°). Keep the frame shaded and closed for about two weeks, after which a chink of air can be admitted. During the third week the cuttings should start rooting and in the fourth week the glass should be removed if growth is by then obvious. Cuttings may be rooted without bottom heat, but this takes longer and more care must be taken to see that they do not damp off.

A horticultural grade of vermiculite, or perlite, may also be used as rooting media, but care must be taken not to get such material too wet. The first potting is into clay or peat fibre pots size about 5cm (2½in) using a suitable potting compost (mixture). When the plants are well rooted they are moved into 8cm (3½in) pots using a similar compost. Later when the plants have produced about eight pairs of fully developed leaves they should receive their first 'stopping'. This means that the leading growth is pinched out to encourage new growths to break at the lower joints. These sidegrowths

Above: the cost of running a stovehouse of this scale would be beyond most amateurs but a selection of tropical plants could be fitted into a section of a greenhouse.
Below: bromeliads do well in the stovehouse.

are later stopped when they are about 15-18cm (6-7in) long. This stopping should not be done all at once, but when the growths are at the right stage. With experience the time of the flowering can be regulated by this means. From the 8cm (3½in) pot stage the plants can be moved on to 10cm (4in) size or straight into 15cm (6in) pots, using a suitable potting compost (mixture). If it is intended to flower the plants for three years grow them in 20cm (8in) pots. Varieties are numerous and as new ones appear regularly it is advisable to consult the descriptive lists issued by specialist growers.

The Stovehouse

This is a greenhouse used for the cultivation of tropical plants and maintained throughout the year at a temperature of about 21°C (70°F), rising with the heat of the sun. A moist atmosphere and ample supply of water, preferably rainwater that has been exposed to the warm air of the house, are necessary; therefore, sizeable water tanks within the house are essential. Most tropical flowering plants require a good light, although some of the decorative

foliage plants may need shading from the hottest sun, and roller-blinds are convenient for this purpose. Ventilation is also an important matter and if this is thermostatically controlled, much labour will be saved as it will be if the heating system is likewise controlled.

Due to the high cost of heating these days, few amateur gardeners can afford to devote a house entirely to stove plants, but a greenhouse can easily be divided off into sections, or into two halves, making the part nearest the source of the heating the stove-end of the house. Or if electricity is being used, then additional tubes can be installed in the stove section.

Plants which require particularly snug conditions may be plunged in a bed or pit, within the house, containing coconut fibre or peat, with heating below to maintain a gentle bottom heat. Many tropical plants make rapid growth and care must be taken not to overcrowd specimens, particularly in the spring and summer, when

growth is at its peak, or they will become drawn and out of character. Also pests, such as mealy bug and mites which multiply rapidly in a high temperature, are more easily controlled. All decaying leaves and plant waste should be carefully removed, as this may harbour pests and diseases.

Fast-growing tropical plants require ample water during the growing season and many of them also require daily overhead syringeing with tepid water which helps to produce a humid atmosphere. However, good drainage is essential whether the plants are grown in pots, tubs or in the border, and an open compost (soil mixture) is necessary so that surplus water can drain away readily. Whether the compost is basically loam or fibrous peat, the addition of sharp silver sand and lumps of charcoal, will improve the drainage and keep the soil sweet.

The most spectacular displays of tropical plants may be seen these

days at botanic gardens, or in the public park departments of the more horticulturally-minded boroughs.

The choice of tropical plants is enormous, orchids alone could fill a large house, and the following lists, which also exclude tropical ferns, give a short selection.

Flowering plants Aechmea, anthurium, aphelandra, begonia, billbergia, bromelia, clerodendrum, clivia, crinum, eucharis, gardenia, hibiscus, hippeastrum, pancratium, plumbago, saintpaulia, strelitzia.

Plants with ornamental foliage Begonia, caladium, croton, dieffenbachia, dracaena, ficus, fittonia, jacaranda, mimosa, peperomia, tradescantia, zebrina.

Climbing plants Allamanda, aristolochia, bougainvillea, cissus, dipladenia, ficus, gloriosa, hoya, ipomoea, jasminum, passiflora, solanum, stephanotis, tecoma.

Crotons (Codiaeums) are striking foliage plants for the stovehouse.

Orchids

Orchids seem to do best if a greenhouse is devoted solely to their cultivation, though some types such as *Odontoglossum grande* and *Coelogyne cristata* will succeed very well in a general collection of plants.

At the outset it is as well to consider the type of orchid collection you desire to grow, or to provide for adding further sections of this large family. A general collection of orchids under one roof containing many species from widely differing habitats is perhaps the most satisfying type of collection. From it you can gain a very broad understanding of the plants. The often wide temperature tolerance of many orchid species makes such a collection possible. Some may wish to establish a collection devoted to perhaps one genus, such as *Cymbidium*.

The ideal method is to divide a small greenhouse into two sections,

Cymbidiums are easy to grow and do not require high temperatures.

one for plants requiring cool conditions, the other for those needing warm conditions. If an existing house is being taken over for orchids, and it provides cool conditions only, a small area could be enclosed with heavy gauge polythene or plastic sheeting, and a soil-warming cable installed. This would allow the growing of warm types in the enclosure and the cool-growing types could be kept in the main body of the house.

The staging or benches, in the house should be of the double type, with a gap of about 15cm (6in) between the upper and lower stages. The upper stage can be of the open wood-slat type for placing the plants on and the under stage should be covered with gravel or ashes. This is referred to as the moisture staging and is frequently sprayed with water to keep up the humidity of the house. A gravel path which can be sprayed is also very useful for this purpose. The type of plant will determine if the staging should be flat or in steps. A wire framework placed on top of the stage, if shaped like a series of step-ladders, will house many more plants if they are hung on the frame. Thin metal rods attached to the main beams of the house just above the path but not over the stage will provide more space, and this system is ideal for the species that prefer more light and many of the smaller orchids.

Ventilators should preferably be under the staging or benches, and in the roof. The ventilators found in many greenhouses in the upright glass sides of the house are not advisable for the orchid house, because draughts are produced and excessive drying out will occur.

There are many heating systems available to the orchid grower today. The once much-favoured boiler-heated water pipes of 10cm (4in) diameter have many advantages including a considerable degree of control. Many efficient electrical systems with thermostatic control are much used and the greenhouse fan type of heater is especially suitable. Care should be taken to install a system capable of providing somewhat above the minimum winter temperature decided on for the particular section of the family grown. Paraffin (kerosene) heating is a controversial subject among orchid growers. Many use this form of heating to provide a supplementary source of heating on very cold winter nights and also for emergencies such as power cuts. Double-glazing with polythene or

plastic sheeting on the inner side of the glass can reduce heat loss and an increase in temperature of five degrees or more has been claimed with the use of double glazing.

A diversity of plants can be managed quite successfully under one roof because, despite attempts to produce uniform conditions in a greenhouse, some parts will inevitably be that much warmer, brighter or moister; and this with a little experimentation, can be turned into a considerable asset. It is well known that with a plant that is reluctant to flower or a slow grower, improved results can be had by moving the plant about the house until it responds to a different environment.

Ventilation

The greater number of cultivated orchids require plenty of fresh air which is essential at all times, especially in the cool and inter-

An orchid house is divided for plants requiring different temperatures.

mediate sections of the orchid house. Besides providing an ample flow of air around the plants, ventilation is also used to help to regulate the temperature. In the warmer orchid houses less air is required as the temperature would be made too low if the house was over-ventilated. Definite rules are difficult to state, but one of the most important is that draughts should be avoided as they can cause more damage than under-ventilating.

The use of top ventilators in the greenhouse roof must depend on the direction of the wind and its force. They should be opened a few centimetres (inches) at first and the opening gradually increased if the temperature rises. Considerable amounts of moisture will be lost if these vents are open for too long. In a small greenhouse, which heats up very quickly, the vents must be opened widely and frequent damping down will be necessary to counteract the moisture loss. Conservation of moisture is most important until the autumn when more air can be admitted to ensure ripening of the plants. The bottom ventilators on the lower sides of the house can be used more frequently, especially if the heating pipes are under the staging. The air entering from these vents is warmed as it passes over the pipes. In the cool and intermediate sections these vents can be left open at night when it is not too cold, and with the cymbidiums a little ventilation can be used on all but the coldest days. If both top and bottom ventilators are to be open at the same time they should be open on the leeward side, which will reduce direct air currents. Usually it is best to open one set of vents only, the top being open when the bottom is closed and vice versa. If the house has ventilators in the glass sides these should not be used as too much moisture would be removed and draughts would be caused.

In general, air should be admitted whenever possible in both summer and winter, provided that excessive moisture and temperature losses are avoided and draughts are not allowed to develop.

Light and shade

Orchids, in general, require plenty of light but not the direct rays of the sun, especially during late spring and summer. Some provision for shading will be required. The application of a shading paint can provide the right density of shading and is easy to apply, but it is more or less permanent until it is removed and it thus provides shade on dull days, when it is required less, as well as on bright days. If the permanent shading is to be used it should be in position by early spring or a little later if conditions are dull. The only really efficient method is to fit movable blinds. These can be of the slatted-wood type or one of the plastic types. Light canvas can be used but does not give such long service.

An air space between the glass and

Above: Cymbidiums are long-lasting and so are popular as cut-flowers.

Below: 'Cambria' one of the many modern hybrids of Cymbidium.

blinds is essential, as this helps to keep a more equable temperature in the house by allowing a free circulation of air over the glass. Blinds other than the wood-slat type, if kept flat on the glass, can cause considerable heating of the glass and hence of the air in the house. Blinds can be usefully lowered in the winter on very cold nights and perhaps even on the very coldest days when a chill wind is blowing, as they give some protection.

Blinds have the great advantage of control; early morning and late evening light can be allowed to reach the plants to their great benefit. On days which are expected to be bright they can be lowered before you leave the house and raised again in the evening. On bright days blinds can be down from about 8 a.m. to 6 p.m. Spring days demand the most caution in the use of blinds when many tender young growths are present on the plants which can very easily be scorched. As the late summer progresses into autumn more light should be admitted: a gradual increase helps to ripen the bulbs and makes the plants generally firm.

Cattleyas, cymbidiums and especially dendrobiums require abundant light to make them flower, while types such as paphiopedilums and masdevallias are definitely shade-loving. Slat blinds, if used for the latter, do not provide the correct density of shade, and hence a very light application of shading paint to the glass will be needed. The blinds can be lowered on the brightest days. This extra shading is also useful as a precaution against damage, should the main blinds be overlooked. In large towns, heavy fog may cause a dark deposit on the glass in winter. This should be washed off, as orchids need all available light at this season.

Feeding
The feeding of orchids is a controversial matter and the beginner is advised not to feed orchids at the start. Plants grown in osmunda composts (mixtures) generally have enough nutriment provided as this material breaks down slowly. The various tree bark composts (mix-

Above: Cattleya 'Clifton Down' a modern hybrid of this large group.

Below: Cattleya loddigesii, *a native of Brazil, is delicately coloured.*

tures) are said to be short of some plant foods, so weak applications of a liquid manure can be given.

Some of the terrestrial types benefit from the addition of old cow manure to the compost (soil mixture). Examples include the deciduous calanthes, thunia, lycaste and phaius. Cymbidiums and paphiopedilums, as well as the genera mentioned, can take regular applications of weak liquid feeds.

If the plants are to be fed, the weakest solution should always be used and then only during the growing season and on plants with a full rooting system. The more feeding a plant receives the more light is necessary. Some climates, such as in Britain for example, do not always provide sufficient light for the ripening of growths, these frequently become soft when they are fed, and then disease troubles develop and the plants do not produce their usual numbers of flowers.

Temperatures

The temperatures for the various sections must be regarded as being average only. During bright spells they may often rise well above the stated maximum. In winter the day temperatures should not be made higher by forcing the heating system.

Warm section In summer a temperature of about 21°C (70°F) by night and 21-27°C (70-80°F) by day, higher during bright spells. In winter 18°C (65°F) by night and 21°C (70°F) by day.

Intermediate section In summer a temperature of about 18°C (65°F) by night and 18-21°C (65-70°F) by day, higher during bright spells. In winter 13-16°C (55-60°F) by night and 16-18°C (60-65°F) by day.

Cool section In summer as near as possible to a temperature of 16°C (60°F) by night and day. In winter by night down to about a temperature of 10°C (50°F) and 13-16°C (55-60°F) by day. Cymbidiums prefer a winter night temperature minimum of 10°C (50°F); this can drop occasionally in very cold spells to 7°C (45°F). In summer by night a temperature as near 10-13°C (50-55°F) as possible and 13-16°C (55-60°F) by day; this can rise to about 21°C (70°F).

'*Lady Coleman*', *a showy hybrid of the epiphytic* Dendrobium *orchids.*

Over-wintering and the resting period

An orchid is resting when it exhibits the least root and top growth activity, usually in winter, and the degree of rest varies considerably in this family of widely differing vegetative types. This makes it impossible to lay down hard and fast rules. In one genus, for example, the species vary one from the other in their requirements. The resting period often corresponds to the dry and either hot or cool period of the plant's native climate. The ideal method for resting orchids is to have a resting house or section, but with a small mixed collection grown under one roof this is not always possible. There is always a cooler end to a greenhouse, however, and this can be used to advantage by placing the resting plants at this end.

Plants without pseudobulbs or tubers must not be rested as they are always active to some extent, and they do not have the food and moisture storage facilities provided by these parts of the plant. Examples of this type include the slipper orchid, paphiopedilum, and the masdevallias. Vandas and aerides and similar types, which have a continuously upward-growing stem, often have thick fleshy leaves which, in nature, are able to resist drought. These plants should receive just enough water to keep fresh the sphagnum moss on the compost surface.

In general, all young unflowered seedlings should be watered at all seasons with due consideration given to the weather. Other orchids with pseudobulbs or tubers require a rest in the winter—generally, the harder the bulb or leaf the longer and drier the rest. Those types that are deciduous or semi-deciduous require a more pronounced rest, for example in the genus *Dendrobium* the *D. nobile* and *D. wardianum* types will take a longer rest than the evergreen types such as *D. thrysifolium*. Most cattleyas and laelias and their hybrids need several weeks rest after flowering. Always keep a look out for shrivelling of the pseudobulbs; a little can be tolerated, but this should never be so extreme as to affect the leading pseudobulb. Ondontoglossums need not be rested in the same way as cattleyas; moisture should always be present to some extent, except for very short periods.

A house containing a small mixed collection will normally have a lower winter temperature and this will help to provide the natural conditions for resting. Attention must mainly be given to the frequency of watering. Careful observation of the individual plant will be the only rule. Failure to rest may induce weak, soft, winter growths, which is always a setback for the plant, and it subsequently takes a long time to regain its former vigour. While reducing the moisture in the greenhouse as a standard winter practice, extreme conditions should be avoided because an excess of dry heat can produce undue shrivelling of the pseudobulbs.

Propagation

The raising of new orchid hybrids from seed is a highly specialized procedure performed under laboratory conditions. The seed is sown on an agar (seaweed) jelly medium containing various mineral salts and sugars.

Seed, glassware and implements are sterilized, as aseptic conditions are essential. After germination, which takes a minimum of three weeks, and may last many months, the seedlings are usually placed onto a fresh agar jelly, again under sterile conditions. After about six months to a year the seedlings are transferred to community pots of standard potting compost (mixture) and placed in the open greenhouse.

Propagation by division is the only method of increasing choice varieties. Paphiopedilums can be split at potting time, making sure that each new piece has several growths including a leading growth. Cattleyas are best treated by severing the rhizome behind the fourth or fifth bulb from the front some months before the plant is to be repotted. A bud on the base of the bulb on the

Pleione 'Oriental Splendour' is a popular, almost hardy terrestrial.

older portion may break into growth, eventually forming a new shoot. These pieces can be potted up separately.

Back bulbs of most orchids can be induced to produce new shoots either as single bulbs or in clusters of two or three. Place these in the warmest position in a pot partly full of crocks and topped with sphagnum moss. Dendrobiums of the nobile section often produce fresh plantlets near the top of old pseudobulbs. These can be taken off with a sharp knife when they have made a few small roots and potted up in the smallest pot available, in pure sphagnum moss. Old back bulbs can be cut up into small pieces of about 5cm(2in) and inserted around the edge of pots filled with moss or sand and peat.

Large plants of many orchids have several leading growths and if these are cut up into pieces with the correct number of bulbs per growth, as many new plants will be formed. Duplication of fine varieties is always advisable against possible loss by accident, but before deciding to break up a large healthy plant the value of such a specimen should be considered. Such plants are very attractive and may receive more attention at shows and other exhibitions. A small propagating frame in the greenhouse greatly facilitates the establishment of plants from bulb divisions and at the same time provides a home for small-growing orchids that require extra warmth.

Pests and diseases

The main pests of orchids are scale insects, mealy bugs, red spider mites and thrips. Scale insects as the name implies, appear as small, brownish or greenish scales on the leaves and stems, especially of cattleyas, where in bad infestations they get behind the bulb sheaths. Control is by sponging or spraying with insecticide. Mealy bugs are small insects covered with a grey meal and can cause considerable damage if allowed to remain unchecked. Like scale insects they also find their way under bracts and leaf sheaths. Small pockets of these insects can be controlled by applying a mixture of nicotine and methylated spirits with a small artist's paint-

Potting materials include Osmunda fibre (top left), sphagnum and crocks.

brush. Red spider mites are small, hardly visible without a hand lens, greenish to red in colour and found on the undersides of the leaves where they cause, in bad infestations, a dry silvered appearance on the leaf surface. They are sucking creatures living on the plant sap. They can be considered to be the worst enemy of the orchid grower as they can transmit virus disease in their passage from one plant to another. Alternation of control sprays is very necessary as resistance to a single spray is soon built up and it will have little effect. Malathion and derris sprays can be used in rotation. Thrips are minute insects and their presence is detected by small round, punctured discoloured areas on the softer leaves and on flowers. The best approach to orchid pests is regular spraying as a preventive measure. Always follow the manufacturer's instructions as some chemicals can be dangerous if due care is not taken. New plants should always be carefully inspected, especially imported plants. Slugs and snails have a taste for fresh young orchid growths as well as roots and flowers. Good control can be effected by using a spray or scattering pellets which can be placed on the benches around the pots.

Diseases are in general uncommon in orchids. Good healthy plants which have been grown under well-aired conditions are seldom attacked. An occasional plant may succumb to black rot disease. Diseased parts can be carefully cut away and powdered sulphur applied to the cut surface. If caught in time this rot can be controlled but very badly infected plant are best destroyed. Virus disease is the one exception. This appears especially in cymbidiums as yellowish streaks or ringed areas which eventually turn blackish. New propagation techniques will ensure that only healthy plants are distributed, while infected plants are best burnt. Control of red spider mites and other sucking insects such as greenfly will reduce the risk of virus spread.

Potting composts (mixtures)

For many years the standard ingredients of orchid potting composts (mixtures) have been osmunda fibre, which is the chopped-up root system of the royal fern (*Osmunda regalis*), and the bog moss known as sphagnum moss. Osmunda fibre is somewhat expensive as it is imported from Italy

and a finer grade from Japan. Though it requires some skill in its use, its long-lasting properties and ability to provide enough food as it breaks down makes it an ideal medium for growing. The beginner would be well advised to gain experience in potting with osmunda fibre and wait until later before experimenting with some of the substitute media. A good general mixture would be 3 parts of osmunda fibre and 1 part of sphagnum moss and for the types requiring more moisture the proportions could be 2-1. Osmunda fibre can be obtained from sone orchid nurseries already prepared and mixed with sphagnum moss for immediate use. This is often available in large quantities, which will make it possible to pot a large number of plants in 10cm (4in) pots. Larger amounts can be bought in the rough state in bales. The bale fibre should be pulled apart, chopped up and the dust sieved out. Selection of the rough and the finer fibres will provide material for those plants with either coarse fleshy roots or thin delicate roots.

The prepared mixture should be neither wet not completely dry but just moist. Prior to a potting session the potting compost should be placed in the greenhouse to keep it warm, as the use of cold material can do damage to the roots by chilling them. Many of the cultivated orchids are epiphytes, that is plants which grow on trees, deriving their nourishment from leafmould and other plant debris which accumulates around the roots and also from the air. They are perching plants only, and do not derive food from their host tree as do the parasitic plants. Many of the roots are freely pendussed in the air and others cling to the bark or penetrate among the mosses which grow along the branches.

The dividing line between the epiphytes and the other group known as the terrestrials is sometimes rather vague. The terrestrial type grows essentially in the soil or in the humus of forest floors. At one time it was the practice to use these two divisions as a guide for potting materials, using fibre and moss for the epiphytes, adding loam fibre to moss and fibre for the so-called terrestrials, such as the plain-leaved slipper orchids (paphiopedilums), cymbidiums and lycastes. The use of loam fibre is not so frequent nowadays, but if good material is available it does help to keep costs down by reducing the amount of osmunda required in the composts.

With care orchids will grow in a wide variety of materials, provided they are of an open texture. For example, various types of tree bark broken down into small pieces are used extensively in the United States. Excellent results are produced, but feeding of some sort seems to be necessary, whereas, with the standard osmunda compost, feeding is not generally necessary. Other substitute or supplementary materials sometimes used are dry bracken fronds, which are said to be rich in potash. Some plastic fibres, which have the same consistency and thickness as osmunda fibre, when mixed with sphagnum moss, give good results with feeding. Even pure sphagnum moss as a potting material has been very successfully used for some orchids.

Bed cultivation of cymbidiums has come into favour and a recently recommended compost (soil mixture) consists of equal parts of leafmould, dry bracken stems, coarse sand, sphagnum peat and old cow dung. This compost (mixture) can also be used for pot cultivation.

Potting procedure

The best time to repot an orchid is generally in the spring or when root growth begins. The plants then have the summer in which to produce abundant roots and complete their growths. If possible, potting should take place when the roots are just showing or at least when they are very short. A plant with long roots is not easy to deal with if damage is to be avoided. The shorter they are the less risk there is of breaking the naturally brittle roots. Potting time must depend on the individual plant, and its growth habits should be studied. Some cattleyas, for example, produce a growth which matures to flowering before roots are formed in abundance, and this is usually in mid summer. Odontoglossums can be

Some orchids can be grown in baskets (top) or rafts (bottom).

potted in spring or in early autumn, at either season avoiding the warmer days when they are making roots. The slipper orchids can be potted after flowering in late winter provided this is done in warm conditions.

In general, orchids need not be potted every year if the compost (potting mixture) remains in a wholesome condition, firm and sweet. If the fingers can be readily pushed into the compost attention is needed. Every other year is a good rule for potting. Even then if the plant has enough room and only a small portion of the compost is soft, the bad part can be replaced with fresh compost, or the surface material can be removed if it is sour and broken down and a top dressing of new compost worked in. Orchids do not like decayed compost but they equally dislike too frequent disturbance and this fact should always be borne in mind when an orchid needs attention; it could be that a drastic treatment such as a complete stripping down of all the

compost would prove fatal. Orchids should never be overpotted, rather they should be underpotted if the correct pot size cannot be used. With the exception of cymbidiums, phaius, *Zygopetalum mackayi* and some of the thick fleshy-rooted types which require ample room to grow, the smallest pot should be chosen. Three-quarter pots or pans are preferable for most types. For those with rambling stems or the pendent or ascending varieties, rafts or baskets would be more suitable. Baskets with widely spaced spars are essential for the stanhopeas which send their spikes downwards, the flowers appearing beneath the container.

The plant to be repotted should be lifted out of its old pot by inserting a potting stick at the back of the plant and gently levering the plant upwards. Where the roots are adhering tightly to the outer surface of the pot less damage can be caused by cracking the pot with a sharp blow.

The new pot should be amply crocked from a third to a half of its depth, depending on type, with pieces of broken pot inserted vertically over the drainage hole. Perfect drainage is essential for orchids. The plant should be prepared by holding it firmly in the left hand, and with a potting stick in the right hand carefully remove downwards all the old soft compost, leaving that which is still sound, especially at the front. Old decayed roots should be cut away to the rhizome and any old soft, brown bulb cut off. This will often allow the plant to be replaced in the same-sized pot. In general, about 4 or 5 bulbs and the new growth should form the plant to be potted, again depending on the individual plant and its vigour. The back part of the plant, that is the oldest bulb, should

1. Use a potting stick to lever a plant from its original pot.
2. Tease the old potting material away from the roots.
3. Work pieces of the new potting material around the roots.
4. Insert the mixture and roots into the pot.
5. Trim the surface of the pots with shears.
6. The potting mixture should be firm without being too tight.

be placed at the rim of the new pot, allowing about 5cm (2in) in front of the leading growth for future development. A small quantity of compost should be placed over the crocks and selected wads of compost (potting mixture) carefully placed about the roots of the plant ensuring a good base beneath the rhizome. Insert the plant into its new pot and carefully work in new compost, starting at the back of the plant and keeping the rhizome level with the top of the pot. The fingers of the right hand should work through the heap of compost, selecting wads of fibres and attempting to gather these so that the wad has the fibres running up and down. This wad should be pressed with a potting stick inwards towards the plant and at the same time slightly downwards. This should continue with the lower level and then with the top layer until the compost level is just below the pot rim. Attention should be given to the inward levering of the compost towards the plant, as any excessive downward pressure can make a caked-hard mass, resulting in impeded drainage. A test for the correct firmness of potting is to pick up the potted plant by the leaves of the bulbs which should not part from the pot. The completed surface can be given a trim with shears. As with all practical matters a demonstration by an expert is the ideal way to learn this essentially simple procedure and such a demonstration can be seen at many orchid nurseries.

Stake the freshly potted plant if necessary and keep it in a shadier place than is usual for the type for some weeks. Attention to the cutting of the osmunda fibre when making up the compost makes for easier potting. It is cut finer for small plants and left in larger pieces if large plants are to be potted.

Watering

The watering of orchids is perhaps the most difficult cultivation procedure for the beginner to understand. Judgement and care must be used. This applies to any pot plant, but orchids do have their special needs. A carefully watered orchid collection can be left for a short time with no ill effect, provided you look after ventilation and shading. Although other plants left for the same time would not be able to withstand the lack of water, this is one of the many advantages in growing orchids.

Rain-water is always preferable to tap water and a tank to receive this, placed in the house, will ensure that the water temperature will be near to that of the house in cold weather. Ordinary tap water, if it is non-alkaline, can be used in some districts. Cold water should never be used. Water well when watering at all; sufficient water should be given to wet the whole of the compost mixture. Never water a wet plant. The timing between waterings will depend on many factors such as the type of orchid, the weather and the temperature. Overwatering is without doubt the main cause of unsuccessful cultivation, the waterlogged compost excludes the air that is so important to the orchid roots. Many beginners take this advice to the extreme and let their plants become tinder dry. This can be equally disastrous except when the type requires a hard dry rest to encourage flowering. This rest is given in the winter. If the drainage is correctly provided and the compost is not too tightly packed—hence of the right porosity —there is less danger of over watering. Perhaps the main cause of damage is too frequent watering. This applies especially when the plants are not in full growth, either early or late in the season and in the winter and also in dull weather when drying out of the compost is not so pronounced. Each plant should be treated as an individual. A watering can with a fine spout is ideal as the amount coming out can be easily controlled when watering plants on the benches. Plants in hanging pots tend to dry out and those in baskets even more so, as they are near glass. They should be immersed in a bucket of water to just over the pot rim.

A well-established plant with a healthy active root system and good drainage in its pot will require liberal watering in its growing season. Recently repotted plants require much less water and are best grouped together at the shadier end of the house. Signs of their need for water are difficult to observe, but if there is any doubt it is best not to water the plant until the following day or when the next general watering takes place. Live sphagnum moss on the compost (potting mixture) surface becomes yellowish when dry and this can be used as a guide that water is required. Lifting the pots (a wet one is obviously heavier than a dry one) does give some indication, especially if this is coupled with feeling the texture of the compost. Another test sometimes used is to pour a little water onto the compost and if this soaks in readily the plant receives no further water. Tapping of the pots as practised with other plants in loam compost is not recommended, as it is both deceptive and unreliable.

Damping down

This is the process of spraying the floors, walls and stages of the orchid house to increase the atmospheric humidity which is so necessary for the continued health of the plants. Greenhouses vary considerably, one being naturally dry and another moist, but as a general rule damping down should be done two or three times a day according to the weather and time of the year, more damping being needed on hot dry days and none on the coldest days.

Damping down is best carried out when the temperature is rising and not when it is falling. Ordinary tap water can be used so as to conserve rain water supplies. Special care is needed in the autumn during mild spells when little heating is being used; the atmosphere can become excessively moist at these times. In winter the greenhouse atmosphere will often become dry due to the greater heat in use. Damping should then be increased slightly but only if the temperature is to be maintained, as any marked decrease in temperature would result in over-moist conditions.

Conclusion

The non-specialist should not be put off growing the less demanding species and varieties. Some of the Pleiones, for instance, can be satisfactorily flowered on a windowsill.

Cacti and other succulents

The growing and collecting of cacti and succulents has been a popular hobby for many years. Their varied shapes and colours together with the coloured spines make them fascinating; and their spectacular flowers are an added interest for the grower. Some of the larger types may not flower without very strong and prolonged sunshine, but many hundreds of other species flower every year. Most cacti come from Mexico and the southern states of the USA, and also from many countries in South America, including Peru, Paraguay, Uruguay, Chile and Brazil. A few are found in the West Indies but none in Africa, India or anywhere in the Far East. As the native habitats of these plants are arid regions it is essential that they be allowed all the sunshine possible to enable them to grow at their best.

Defining cacti

All cacti are succulents but not all

A small succulent collection can include varied shapes and colours.

succulents are cacti. Spines are found on all true cacti and these spines grow from a small tuft of hair or wool. This is known as an areole and no other plant has it. No cacti have leaves except the genus *Pereskia*. This plant has areoles and leaves and also a multiple flower, unlike true cacti which have a simple, or single flower. The flowers of cacti have no

stem or stalk, the ovary being connected directly with the plant. Exceptions to this rule are the pereskias.

The flowers of most cacti are formed at the areole but a few genera produce flowers away from this point. Plants of the genus *Mammillaria* produce their flowers at the axil, the spot between the tubercles. This genus also makes new plants or offsets at the axil as well, whereas most cacti make offsets at an areole. The flowers of cacti vary considerably in size from 8mm ($\frac{1}{2}$in) in some mammillarias to 35cm (14in) across in some of the night-flowering types. The larger flowers may not be produced in profusion; but some of the cacti with smaller flowers can have rings of flowers all around the top of the plants for months at a time.

Cacti are often described as desert plants but this is not quite true. Many are found in prairie-type country where there may be a few small trees and shrubs with coarse grasses intermingled. Some are found in good loam while others are found growing on rocks and the mountain side. Some of the best flowering cacti, the epiphyllums, grow in the forests of Brazil, usually on trees. Such cacti are classed as epiphytes or epiphytic cacti.

Larger specimens make an attractive display in a specialized glasshouse.

Cultivation

As cacti vary so much in size from perhaps 2.5cm to 9m (1in to 30ft) or more, there are many species available to the grower to suit almost any situation or conditions. The best place to grow a collection of cacti is in a sunny greenhouse, although there are many kinds that can be grown quite well in a sunny window.

Although all cacti can go for long periods without water, it is essential that they are provided with an adequate supply during the growing period or they cannot flourish.

To grow cacti well and flower them it is imperative to provide them with a porous soil as the roots soon rot if they are wet for days on end. Many types of potting soils (mixtures) have been used and recommended, even different ones for each genus; it is possible, however, to grow practically all types of cacti in one kind of potting mixture. The art of growing cacti is in the watering and the amount given can vary according to the type of mixture. Plants can only obtain their nourishment in a liquid form and so if little water is given the plant cannot obtain much food.

Potting composts (mixtures)

A very good potting compost for cacti may be made up from a compost with a few added nutrients, to which is added a sixth part of coarse sand to make it more porous. Some additions of broken brick or granulated charcoal may be incorporated in the added sand. If it is desired to mix a compost for general use, the following will be found quite reliable. Take two parts of loam, one part of peat and one part of sharp, coarse sand. Mix well and to each bushel add 20g ($\frac{3}{4}$oz) of ground chalk or limestone, 20g ($\frac{3}{4}$oz) sulphate of potash, 40g ($1\frac{1}{2}$oz) of superphosphate and 40g ($1\frac{1}{2}$oz) of hoof and horn grist. All the globular and columnar types of cacti may be grown in this medium, while for the epiphytes some slightly heavier type of potting mixture may be used, as these plants will benefit from the richer soil. The very spiny types of cacti do not require heavy feeding with fertilizers and as long as they are repotted at least every two years they will grow quite well. If these plants are fed too liberally they will become lush, open in texture, and be very liable to rot off in the winter. Also it will be found that the spines formed when the plant has been fed with fertilizers may not be as stout and well coloured as when the plant had been grown harder. When making up the cactus compost (mixture) it is very important to find a good loam as a basis for the mixture. An ideal type is the top spit from an old-standing meadow. Unfortunately these meadows are becoming few and far between and the loam is often only the under spit after the top turf has been removed. The peat is not so important but the sand must be very sharp and coarse. Silver sand is useless for cactus compost and the type known as washed grit, or river grit, is the best.

The potting medium should not be used immediately after it has been mixed and a lapse of two weeks at least is desirable before potting. The time to repot varies considerably, and depends on many factors. Some cacti are very slow growers and so may be left in their pots for two or three years while others may need a move twice a year. Many cacti never flower because they have been in the same stale, worn-out soil for many years. With fairly frequent watering during the growing period the roots of the plant use up the nourishment in the soil, and clearly there can be little food value left in it after about a year.

Repotting

The best time for repotting is during the growing period, which with most cacti will be between March and September. Once new growth is seen on a plant it can be repotted. When dealing with a fairly large collection it will be found better to make a start with the larger pots. These can then be cleaned for use with other plants which may need a bigger pot. It is also a good plan to make a clear place in the greenhouse and place all repotted plants there so that none is missed. The pots should be clean and well crocked. It is unnecessary to place a large number of crocks in the pot as they will only take up valuable space which would be better occupied by good soil. The best way to crock a pot for a cactus is to cut as large a piece of broken flower pot as will lie in the bottom of the pot. This large crock will then form a kind of platform when the plant is removed the next time. If a stick is pushed up through the drainage hole the crock will force the whole ball of soil up in the pot, whereas if a number of small pieces of crock are used it is possible to damage the roots when trying to remove the plant another time.

Place some of the coarsest particles of medium over the crock and then a little soil. Remove the plant from the old pot and hold it by the root system. Gently work all the old soil away from the roots. If any appear dead they should be cut away. Now rest the plant in the pot and gradually work in some fresh mixture.

Prepare a well-crocked pot with a porus potting material (1 and 2) before sowing cactus seed (3). A pot can be divided to distinguish seedlings of different species and varieties (4 and 5). Use a spoon to pot up larger specimens (6 and 7). Grafting (8) is a useful way of assisting growth of the slower growing kinds.

Because most of the plants are spiny it may not be possible to work the soil in with the hands as is possible with ordinary plants. A tablespoon can be used to insert the soil and it can be gently firmed in with an old table-knife handle. A wooden stick must not be used as it would catch in the spines and break them. Once a spine is broken it will never grow again. See that the plant is in the same relative position in the soil as it was before. See also that a space of at least 12mm ($\frac{1}{2}$in) is left at the top of the pot for watering. The plant should look right in the new pot; do not use one too large so that the plant looks lost or yet one so small that there is no room for soil as well as the base and roots of the plant. For the globular kinds of cacti a pot which is 12mm ($\frac{1}{2}$in) bigger all around than the plant will do for pots up to 88mm ($3\frac{1}{2}$in) in diameter, but for a larger plant a pot at least 25mm (1in) larger all round must be provided. This will not be sufficient for many of the taller-growing types as the pot must be large enough to form a firm base to stop the plant and pot from falling over.

Plastic pots may be used, especially for small plants; they do not appear to dry out as quickly as clay pots. Once the plant is potted it is important to insert the label, and a good plan is to put the date of repotting on the back. This is a useful guide in a large collection. As it is essential that the soil should be able to discharge all surface water as soon as possible, the pots should not be stood on a flat surface. Some coarse gravel makes an ideal base on which to stand the pots. If slats are provided in the greenhouse it is better to cover them with corrugated asbestos sheeting on which the gravel may be placed. Any plants stood on shelves must have a saucer containing gravel under them to allow the free removal of surplus water.

Watering cacti

Watering the plants presents the most important part of cactus culture. More plants are lost through overwatering than from any other cause. As has been stated before, cacti will not grow without water but if they

get too much they can soon die. Newly potted cacti should not need watering for about a week. The potting soil should have been crumbly moist at the time of moving the plant. If it is too wet or too dry it cannot be firmed in the correct manner. The whole secret of watering can be described in one sentence. Never water a plant if the soil is still damp. It is not easy to tell when a cactus needs watering. Ordinary plants soon show by drooping leaves when water is required, but cacti cannot show their needs in this way. Therefore, it is necessary to feel the surface of the soil to see if it is dry. This should be done in the morning, when the soil will be of uniform dampness. Evening inspections may be misleading as

Mammillaria geminispina, *an attractive member of a large group.*

after a hot day for example, the surface soil will be dry while that at the base of the pot is still moist.

Rainwater is better than tap water but if rainwater is not available let some tap water stand in the open for a day or two before it is used. Water may be given from a can with a small spout so that it can be directed into any pot. Do not water by immersion except for the first watering after the winter. If plants are watered this way often, all the nourishing matter will soon be washed out of the pot. Cacti may be sprayed in the evening of a hot day. No water need be given from the end of September to early

March. Then water when the soil has dried out, not before. The Christmas cactus, *Zygocatus truncatus*, may be watered during the winter as long as the temperature is not below 10°C (50°F). Other cacti may be left at 4°C (40°F), so that they get a winter's rest.

Propagation

Propagation is by cutting, taking offsets or by seed raising.

Taking cuttings Cuttings taken from opuntias and epiphyllums are removed with a sharp knife and the cut part is allowed to dry in the sun. The cuttings are then rested on a mixture of equal parts of peat and sharp sand (not silver sand). Cactus potting compost (mixture) may be used to fill three-quarters of the pot, with the rooting medium on top. Place in a sunny position and spray occasionally. Too much water must not be given until roots have formed. Tall cuttings will have to be supported by a stick, as they must not be pushed into the medium.

Grafting Grafting may be done to assist the growth of a small, slow-

Above: the ribbed body of Ferocactus acanthodes *is caged in spines.*
Below: the tiny plantlets of Bryophyllum tubiflorum *form on leaf ends.*

growing type. A tall type is used for the stock, such as *Trichocereus spachianus*. The top is cut from the stock where the growth is new and healthy. The scion is cut at the base so that it is about the size of the top of the stock. It is brought in contact with the freshly cut stock and kept in position with two small weights on a piece of string, pressing the scion down firmly. Keep in the shade for a week or two and a small joint will form.

Raising cacti from seed Some cacti never make offsets and these have to be raised from seed. A small propagating frame can easily be made and heated with an electric cable or even an electric lamp. Half-pots of about 10cm (4in) in diameter are very good for sowing small quantities of seed. They can even be divided with celluloid labels if more than one species is to be sown in the pot. Use a light seed compost (mixture) and sieve a small quantity through a perforated zinc sieve. Place the coarse material over the crock, then top up with ordinary mixture, and put 2.5cm (1in) of the fine soil on top. Small seed must not be buried, but fairly large seeds can be just pushed into the soil. Water the first time by standing in con-

Lobivias, cactus plants from Bolivia, have comparatively large flowers.

grower wishes to experiment, he should make sure that any cacti left out during the winter are those that can be parted with, and not specimen plants.

All the spiny types of cacti can stand a great deal of sunshine as long as there is plenty of air available in a greenhouse. The epiphytes benefit from shade during the hotter months of the year, and may be stood outside the greenhouse provided no frosts are forecast. Cacti kept in windows of the house must be where they can get the maximum amount of light and they will not flower well unless they can get a fair amount of sunshine. Most cacti flower in spring, summer or autumn, and it will be found that many flower on new growth only. If the flowers are pollinated many colourful seed pods can be formed. On the mammillarias these pods can look very attractive.

Pests

If cacti are grown well they suffer little disease but there are a few pests that may attack a sick plant. The most frequent one is mealy bug. This appears in a small tuft of wool or powder. Scale may also attack some cacti and looks like a small scab. Red spider may be a nuisance if the atmosphere is too dry. All these pests can be killed with malathion, used as directed on the bottle.

Succulents

The growing of succulent plants is much easier than the cultivation of most pot plants. These plants are found in nature in districts where there is either little rainfall or the rain is limited to two or three months in the year, and so they are able to withstand considerable drought. By the composition of their skin covering they can conserve the moisture in their leaves or stems and do not wither or droop when they do not get watered. All cacti are succulents, but the other succulents have no areoles as have the cacti. They also have leaves, which are carried by only two or three genera in the *Cactaceae*.

There are so many different genera

tainers of water so that the whole soil can be well moistened. Place in the frame with a piece of glass on top and then cover with dark paper. The best time to sow is in early spring, in a temperature of 21°C (70°F); seeds will germinate at a lower temperature but will take longer to do so. Once seedlings have appeared, the paper must be removed and the glass should be raised slightly. The seedling must be kept from the direct sun for the first year but they must have plenty of light or they will become drawn. Do not allow the seed pots to dry out while germination is taking place; watering may be done with a fine spray.

Prick out when the cotyledon has been absorbed. Before this the root is so tiny that it can be broken very easily, in which case the seedling would die. The seedlings may be placed 2.5cm (1in) apart in the cactus compost (mixture) as described above. Do not pot up too soon into small pots as these dry out very quickly. Boxes made of concrete or plastic are better for the seedlings until they are ready to go into 5cm (2in) pots.

Summer treatment

Cacti may be planted out in beds from June to September. If they are removed from their pots it may be quite impossible to put them back in the same sized pots in the late summer or autumn. They may be left in their pots, but the drainage hole must be freed from soil when they are removed. A few cacti may stand the winter out of doors but a very severe winter could possibly kill some. If the and species of succulents that it is not possible to deal with them all here, but only to make some general observations. South Africa is the home of very many of the genera grown by collectors, although America also has very many species. Many collectors of cacti have some other succulents among them.

Special treatment

As most succulents thrive in the same conditions, it is necessary to give only the few exceptions special treatment to be able to grow them all in one greenhouse. Those which may present some difficulty in a mixed collection are the 'mimicry' types which are found in South Africa. Many of these have a particular resting period and unless this is copied in cultivation it is probable that the plants will grow out of character. Those mimicry plants of the mesembryanthemum group, such as lithops and conophytums, are better placed by themselves in the greenhouse where they can be given specially required treatment with regard to watering, etc. Some succulents do not require as much sunshine as others. It may be possible to site these in the greenhouse where they are able to get partial shade, perhaps from taller-growing plants.

Some of the plants which do not do too well in direct sunshine are the gasterias and haworthias. These turn very red or bronzed and may cease to grow in too much sunshine. In their native habitats they do not grow in the hot, dry season. It is only when the rains come that they make any new growth and flower. It is probable that in some regions where many succulents grow there may be no rainfall for a year or two.

If the natural conditions of their native habitats are understood it will be easier to provide the necessary treatment for the successful growth of succulents. However, although these plants grow in so many different climatic regions, and in spite of the special treatment required by some types, it is possible to grow most kinds quite successfully by the same method of treatment and in the same soils.

Soil and compost

Most succulents are not at all particular as to the type of soil they are grown in provided it is porous. Many can be grown in almost pure sand, while some grow better in a fairly rich compost (mixture) as long as drainage is good.

It is sometimes recommended that a special soil be used for each genus, but it is possible to grow a varied collection by using one soil only. If you have a large number of plants to pot up, you will, no doubt, like to mix your own soil; but where only a few plants are to be dealt with it is far easier to buy a commercial potting compost (mixture) and just add a little extra roughage to make up a suitable compost, or make your own according to the method given previously for cacti.

The standard well-drained potting compost (mixture) has larger proportions of loam and peat to sand than has the mixture recommended previously. Although this is excellent for ordinary plants it will be found that it holds too much moisture to be suitable for the succulents. Some need a more porous soil than others, but by adding the necessary roughage it is possible to use commercial potting mixes for all types.

By adding the extra roughage the proportion of fertilizers will be lessened; but few succulents require a rich mixture. If a mixture is used which is too rich in added fertilizers

Bergeranthus multiceps *is a highly succulent plant for the greenhouse.*

it is probable that the plants will grow out of character. They may then become soft and sappy and succumb to cold, wintry conditions.

Repotting

The time for repotting depends on the type. With kinds that have a resting period it is necessary to wait until new growth has begun before repotting. Normally, March would be the time for this task but the genus may be resting then and so must wait for a few months before being repotted. Most succulents will probably benefit from a repotting at least every two years. Any plant in a small pot which is watered occasionally will have used up most of the nourishment in the soil and so will need a change. Some of those that grow more rapidly can be repotted once a year. If the plant growth reaches the side of the pot a larger pot is needed. It is important to be able to inspect the actual soil in the pot to decide whether or not the plant needs watering. All the old soil must be discarded. A good crock should almost cover the drainage hole of the pot; the larger it is the easier it will be to remove the plant when repotting again becomes necessary. The compost (medium) should be crumbly moist when potting is done, and then, as with cacti, no water need

be given for about a week or more, depending on how long the soil takes to dry out.

Watering

Once watering is begun in the early part of the year, enough should be given each time to ensure that all the soil in the pot is well damped. It may be necessary to go over all plants again to ensure that enough has been given. Most ordinary pot plants will soon indicate when water is needed by their drooping leaves. This sign is not apparent with the succulents even after weeks without watering and so, if you wish to grow the plants successfully, you must not wait for the leaves to droop but water frequently and regularly. But remember that succulents will not survive for long in a waterlogged soil, so adequate drainage is essential.

The secret of watering all succulents is to refrain from giving any more water until the soil has dried out. This depends on the warmth of the greenhouse and the plants' rate of growth. As with cacti, more succulents are lost by over-watering than are lost by under-watering. The method of watering by immersion is not to be recommended unless the

Tropical cacti such as Rhipsalis rosea *'Electra' need rich and moist soil.*

soil in the pot has become very dry. If plants are repeatedly immersed most of the nourishment in the soil will be washed out of the drainage hole. When a pot is lifted from deep immersion much dirty water, containing a lot of soluble food, will run out of the bottom. Constantly watering in this way will mean that there will be nothing left in the soil of much use to the plant.

One method of watering a very dry pot is to place the plant pot in a receptacle and pour only a very small amount of water into the receptacle. This must only be as much as the soil can absorb completely, and when the pot is lifted no water should run out of the bottom. Some composts (mixtures) are very difficult to wet especially after the long dry winter rest. A teaspoonful of detergent in a gallon of water will help to moisten the root ball thoroughly.

Propagation

Some succulents can be raised from seed and soon make sizeable plants, others can be propagated by division or by taking cuttings. Many of the succulent-leaved types can be increased by taking off the leaves and rooting them in sharp sand. Where this is done the leaves should just be laid on the surface of the sand. If leaves or cuttings are pushed into the sand too deeply rot may set in causing failure to root.

Summer and winter treatment

Some of the succulents which do not like excessive summer heat in the greenhouse may be placed out of doors from June to early September. They must be protected from slugs, etc. Water them occasionally during dry weather. If these plants are bedded out for the summer it will be difficult to repot them into the same sized pots when they are removed. For many plants it is better to leave them in their pots when they are put outside.

Most succulents can be kept at 4-7°C (40-45°F) through the winter provided the soil is dry, and they can stand any temperature they are likely to encounter in the greenhouse during the summer.

Ferns

Considerable confusion exists in the mind of the non-botanist gardener between true ferns, of which there are probably some 10,000 or more species in the world, and so-called ferns such as *Asparagus sprengeri*. True ferns consist of roots, stems and leaves but no flowers and are always recognizable by the brownish or blackish patches or sori (singular, sorus) found on the underside of the fully grown leaf. The sori are in most ferns covered by an indusium (plural, indusia) which is an outgrowth from the surface of the leaf, and is of extreme importance in identifying the genus of the fern. Each sorus consists of a group of sporangia (singular, sporangium) which are filled with powdery spores from which new plants can be propagated.

The roots of ferns are always fibrous and many species have rhizomes and creeping stems either just at or on the soil surface. The leaves arise directly from the rhizomes, sometimes in tufts in a wastepaper basket formation and sometimes altnately along the creeping stems, which over the years appears to give some ferns the ability to move.

The half-hardy kinds may be grown indoors or in a conservatory or greenhouse, unheated during the summer months and where the frost can be kept away in winter with a minimum temperature of 4°C (40°F). Shading from the direct rays of the sun is an absolute necessity and daily syringeing to maintain a moist atmosphere keeps the fronds plump and fresh. Tender or hot-house ferns need similar conditions but higher temperatures; not falling below 16°C (60°F) in the winter. All greenhouse ferns have a period of dormancy when they require much less water, but must not be dried off completely. During this time they like to be kept cooler, and the atmosphere can be much more buoyant. Ventilation is perhaps the most important single factor in fern houses, and if some bottom ventilation can be given, draughts are avoided and the atmosphere does not dry out as quickly. Daily syringeing with a really fine

Black spleenwort can be grown outdoors or in greenhouse conditions.

spray (of all but the hairy kinds or those covered with farina) and continuous damping down of the staging and walls helps to maintain the humidity required.

Attractive arrangements can be created in quite modest fern houses by the construction of stone 'walls' or beds, using bark and peat blocks to soften the effect. Fern baskets or fern pots shaped like bowls can be suspended from the rafters, and plants in these will need greater attention to watering than those planted among the stones or in pots plunged into the borders.

Climbing ferns make an attractive addition but need more space.

Propagation
In spring when the ferns are repotted and just as new growth begins to swell, a plant can be divided and the divisions potted up separately and kept close until growth is evident. Creeping ferns can be increased by cutting off a piece of the rhizome with frond buds and potting it up separately. Some ferns, for example Aspidium (shield fern), occasionally produce small plants on the fronds. These can be pegged down into pots or boxes of fine compost (soil mixture) and severed after rooting has taken place.

The most interesting method of propagation is by sowing the spores that are produced in the spore cases (sporangia) on the backs of the fronds. Put a mature frond into a white envelope for a few days to dry off and collect the powdery spores.

Asparagus fern, A. plumosus, though not a true fern, goes well with them and with many flowering plants.

Sow these on the surface of sandy compost (mixture), previously sterilized, in a pan first half filled with crocks. Stand the pan in shallow water, cover it with glass or polythene and shade. Autumn sowing is best but the spores may be saved until the spring. The resulting green plant, or prothallus, bears no resemblance to the original fern but is the sexual generation in the life cycle of the fern. The prothalli should be put into a pan or box about 2.5cm (1in) apart, just pressed on to the soil, and the resulting tiny fern plants potted up individually once they are big enough to handle.

The alpine house

Quite different in purpose from most other types of greenhouse, a proper alpine house is little more than a means of protecting, from extremes of weather, plants which are among the hardiest when growing in their natural environment. Though we rarely experience the low temperatures which occur in alpine regions, our comparatively mild winters are not enjoyed by high alpine plants.

This is because in their natural habitat, during their winter resting period, they are usually snugly hidden under a layer of snow which acts as insulation against extreme cold and, most important, keeps them comparatively dry. The chief purpose of an alpine house is, therefore, to prevent uncontrolled moisture, an excess of which usually leads to rotting, from reaching the plants

An alpine house is a useful way to display small plants, including bulbs.

during their resting period.

Alpine plants, some delicate in cultivation, can be given individual needs in separate containers in full control of the grower within the alpine house. The first consideration is usually a growing mixture similar to that in which the plants grow in the wild, together with proper drainage, shading, etc. Such conditions are not so easily arranged in the open. There is also the question of plants which flower in the depth of our winter being damaged by wind or heavy rain. Well known among these are the Engleria and Kabschia saxifrages. *Narcissus bulbocodium romieuxii* and early primulas—*P. allionii* and *P. edgeworthii*. The protection of the alpine house allows them to remain unspoiled by rough weather.

The grower has the advantage of being able to study the plants at a convenient level on the staging, no matter what the weather conditions outside. Further, not all the collection need be housed together. Specimens can be kept in special frames attached to the outside, and taken in for viewing when they are at their best.

Shading

Though alpine houses are made to allow maximum ventilation, the addition of shading is needed to break

Right: campanulas, such as C. isophylla, *are good alpine house plants.*
Below: the Pasque flower, Pulsatilla vulgaris, *flowers at Easter.*

the direct rays of the sun while it is at its strongest in late spring and summer. It helps further to keep the house cool and can be applied in a number of ways. Commercial washes have the serious disadvantage of being semi-permanent and cannot be easily removed during dull spells. Shading in position during prolonged dull periods can irreparably damage alpine plants by causing them to become drawn, due to insufficient light, a condition from which they seldom recover (many are of compact cushion-forming habit).

Shading is best done by means of one of the various kinds of adjustable blinds made either of plastic material or of laths.

Heating

Many purist alpine growers would object to the use of heat in the house, in any form. The fact is, however, that when used with discretion by

Above: gentians are among the choicest of all alpine plants.

Below: the shooting star, Dodecatheon meadia, *needs cool, conditions.*

the amateur it can save losses, in just the same way as other adjustments are made to the plant environment for the same purpose. The house prevents direct rainfall onto the plants but little can be done to control atmospheric humidity, which becomes very high during dull, dark and foggy spells. The 'woolly' plants are among the first to suffer in these conditions. A little heat during such times can help to dry the air in the house.

Again, the usual method of plunging the plant containers in a base of chippings can allow severe prolonged cold to penetrate and freeze roots which would, in nature, be too deeply situated for this to happen. In their natural environment the plants would also have the added protection of an insulating layer of snow over them, which they lack in the alpine house. Even where their root systems can stand being frozen, evergreens are liable to perish through being unable to take up moisture continually being lost from the foliage. A little heat can prevent all this.

Plant collection

A properly built alpine house is not essential to enable a keen gardener to enjoy growing a few alpine plants, though the conditions described should be provided as nearly as possible for easier kinds to be tried.

Cushion-forming plants are perhaps the most typical grown, and a start could be made with a selection from the wide choice of mossy saxifrages. No collection would be complete without representatives of the many species of bulbous plants which provide lovely miniature blooms often of the original parents of our much larger garden hybrids—narcissus and tulips for example. Others include species iris, fritillarias, galanthus (snowdrops) and scillas (squills). Most of these are best kept in frames when out of bloom.

Small shrubs provide added interest and often permanent evergreen features among the plants in an alpine house. The dwarf conifers are well known and are obtainable in all shapes from rounded to spire-like in habit, typified by the popular juniper, *Juniperus communis compressa.*

Vegetables under glass

In cooler climates, a greenhouse—even a small, unheated one—is an extremely useful addition to a kitchen garden. It has two important functions for the vegetable grower. Firstly, it gives permanent protection to tender crops that need a degree of warmth or constant shelter to grow successfully; tomatoes, cucumbers, and most winter salads are common examples. Secondly, it can act as a temporary home for young plants (propagated from seed or from cuttings) until such time as they have reached a suitable size for planting out and the weather is warm enough. Temporary protection is commonly given to many vegetables liable to frost damage in the early stages, and to those that will crop earlier if given an early start under glass. Sweet corn, aubergine (eggplant), sweet pepper, and similar tender crops are also often pot-grown under

Tomatoes are popular and very reward-ing vegetables to grow under glass.

glass and transplanted to a warm site outdoors when all danger of frost has passed.

A single greenhouse can, of course, be used for both these purposes. Indeed, if there is some artificial warmth installed for a permanent crop, it is wise to make most use of the heat available. However, artificial heating is not essential and, if economy is vital, you can wait before starting your more tender crops in the greenhouse until the weather naturally provides sufficient warmth—this is earlier than most people think.

There are many advantages to owning a greenhouse. You can save money by growing your own tomatoes, cucumbers, sweet peppers, melons and other crops that are expensive to buy in the shops, and you can raise your own vegetable seedlings cheaply from seed. You can also grow out-of-season crops like early tomatoes and winter salads. Again, these are normally very costly if bought from shops. As well as saving a great deal of money, you will find that vegetables grown in your greenhouse have an appearance, texture, aroma and flavour that only come with absolute freshness.

Making the most of your greenhouse

To make the best use of a greenhouse devoted to vegetables, crop growing schedules should be planned so that as crops are harvested, others can be sown or planted to take their place. Catch cropping should be practised where possible. For example, radishes or carrots demand little room and can usually be fitted in between rows of other slower-growing crops requiring more space. It is also wise to make the most of the height a greenhouse has to offer. Too often you see a greenhouse devoted to quite low-growing salad crops that could just as well be grown in frames.

If it makes good use of space, there is no objection to using most vegetable houses for growing a few decorative plants. However, it is possible for many such plants to carry virus diseases and they may transfer these to your crops, although they may not show any symptoms themselves.

A large number of different kinds of vegetables can be grown in a greenhouse which is gently heated in the winter. With more heat the list becomes longer, and you can also grow crops out of season. Many of these vegetables, however, can be grown equally successfully in frames

or under cloches, and these may prove to be more economical methods of growing them. Some vegetables are not at all suitable for greenhouse cultivation, such as the runner bean, which does not do well under glass because it pollinates well only in the open.

Cucumbers do well in the base-wall type greenhouse when grown in pots on the staging (benches) and supported by wires (pages 67-72). Generally, tomatoes should not be grown together with cucumbers because they require different conditions (cucumbers prefer more shade and a much more humid atmosphere) and many of the pesticides that can be used safely on tomatoes will harm cucumbers. However, it is not impossible to achieve good results by growing both crops in the same house, provided that you choose a suitable variety of cucumber, such as Conqueror, which will tolerate the sort of conditions under which tomatoes thrive.

Mushrooms are a good fill-in crop for a heated greenhouse where there is a staging, since they can be grown

below it. Alternatively, you can use the space beneath the staging in winter for forcing vegetables such as asparagus, rhubarb, seakale or chicory—this will involve blacking out the area under the staging by means of black polythene sheeting.

Even if you do not want to devote your greenhouse entirely to the cultivation of vegetables, it can be used to start them from seed early in spring or, in a heated house, to force early crops. But there are certain vegetables, such as tomatoes, cucumbers and lettuce, which give rewarding crops if a greenhouse is given over solely to their cultivation.

Tomatoes

Tomatoes have always been one of the most popular crops for the amateur gardener. Once regarded almost solely as a greenhouse crop, with the development of new hardier varieties many people now grow them successfully outdoors. How-

A well-shaped truss of tomatoes ripening in early summer.

ever, it is important to remember that the crop is native to a fairly hot, dry climate. High summer temperatures suit tomatoes perfectly, but since that kind of weather cannot be expected every year in a temperate climate, some care must be taken to give them the right situation. Cloches and frames can be used in several different ways to give you a better chance of a good outdoor crop.

Tomatoes in a cold greenhouse
Most gardeners save growing time by starting tomato plants under glass, even if they are to be transplanted outdoors later. There is no doubt that a greenhouse gives the very best conditions for a successful crop.

Soil
Tomatoes will grow in almost any reasonably rich soil, even in a basically poor soil if plenty of nutrients are supplied during the season. A greenhouse border soil can be prepared for tomatoes by flooding with water about a month before planting to ensure good water reserves in the subsoil (this is very important) and then, when the soil is workable, by working in rotten organic matter such as farmyard manure at the rate of one barrowload per 3.5sq m (per 4sq yd). About 7/10 days before planting, fork into the top few inches a dressing of a commercial tomato fertilizer at the rate recommended by the makers. However, after a few years of growing tomatoes in the same soil, pests, bacteria and fungi will multiply in a greenhouse, so precautions must be taken. Either sterilize the soil each year or introduce new compost. A home-made compost can be made of four parts good, sieved loam (preferably a fairly heavy one), one part well-rotted farmyard manure or garden compost, one part coarse sand (all parts by bulk), together with 125g (4oz) of a tomato fertilizer, and 22g ($\frac{3}{4}$oz) lime per bushel of mixture. Mix together well, and leave for ten days before use.

Isolate this compost from the soil of the greenhouse floor by growing the plants in boxes or containers separated from the ground by staging or a sheet of polythene.

An increasingly popular method is

Tomatoes can be sown in propagators from late winter on.

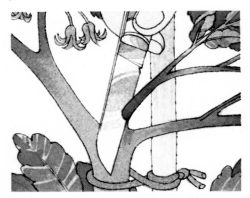

Use a clean knife to remove axillary shoots from single-stem varieties.

to use 'grow-bags', which are polythene sacks filled with a suitable compost. Normally bought complete and ready for use from garden supply centres, they prevent the tomato roots coming into contact with contaminated soil.

Sowing
Sow the seed in boxes, pots or trays of well-draining sieved loam or seed compost from mid-winter to early spring. Sow each seed separately, about 0.5cm ($\frac{1}{4}$in) deep and 2.5cm (1in) apart. Cover the seed-box with glass and brown paper or black polythene until the seeds start to germinate in about 7–14 days. Then remove the covering and expose the seedlings to as much light as possible without burning them.

Tomatoes require a germination temperature of about 15°C (60°F). That temperature should be maintained, if possible, throughout the life of the plant; 10°C (50°F) is about the lowest permissible level. 27°C (80°F) is generally considered to be the upper limit. If you are sowing

Prick seedlings off as soon as they are large enough to handle.

Transplant to permanent beds when plants are about 15 cm (6 in) high.

before spring, sow more seed than you might think necessary. This earlier sown seed has a tendency to produce a percentage of inadequate, fern-like plants with ragged leaves—because of poor light. These must be rejected, as they will never crop well.

Transplanting
Transplanting is done in two stages. When the seedlings have grown two seed leaves, and the first true leaf is starting to appear, they need to be moved to give them more growing space. It is usual to transplant them into 7.5cm (3in) pots, often into peat pots or pots made of black polythene, containing a suitable potting compost (soil mixture) for tomatoes. The young plants remain in the pots, in maximum light, to grow into strong, bushy specimens. When they are 12.5–15cm (5–6in) high they are ready to transplant into their permanent bed, which in the greenhouse can be a pot, box or grow-bag, or a border in the greenhouse floor. At this stage each plant will probably have its first truss of flowers beginning to open.

Single-stem tomatoes need support if they are to bear the weight of a good crop.

A wide range of tomatoes is available, including heavy-cropping, yellow-fruited varieties.

Single-stem varieties are generally used for greenhouse cultivation; bush varieties are best under cloches (Hotkaps).

Varieties of plum tomato make an attractive alternative to the more common medium round.

When transplanting. handle carefully, keeping the soil in a ball around the roots. Make sure that both the soil around the plants and the soil into which they are to be set are thoroughly damp, but not saturated. Dig a hole large enough to take the entire contents of the pot in which the plant has been growing. Fill the hole with water if the weather is very dry and quickly transfer the plant and its surrounding compost into it. Press the soil firmly around the stem.

Support

Well-grown tomatoes should yield 3.5–5.5kg (8–12lb) of fruit per plant in a season. This is a heavy weight for a plant with a thin stem, so the plant needs support. A string (3 or 4-ply fillis) may be suspended for each plant from an overhead wire, attached at the lower end to a wire hook plunged into the soil, about 23cm (9in) deep, or to a wire running horizontally about 3.5cm (1½in) above the soil, along the row of plants. As the plant grows the string is twisted gently around it taking great care not to snap the top of the plant.

Ventilation and shading

Adequate ventilation is essential—stagnant air allows diseases to develop. Open doors and ventilators as much as possible, avoiding draughts to the plants. Attempts to save on heating costs by keeping ventilators closed may result in attacks of moulds and mildews, which thrive in stuffy atmospheres. It is better to keep the plants well aired, albeit slightly chilly, even though this may mean a slightly later crop.

Provide shade for the plants whenever the temperature rises above 27°C (80°F), by painting the glass with a commercial shading compound—there is one which is opaque in sunny weather, and translucent in rain. Alternatively a mixture of quicklime in enough water to make it milk-like, with a little size added for sticking, can be used. You may of course have Venetian or roller blinds (window shades) attached to the ridge outside the greenhouse which can be used as needed, on the south side. Without shading, leaves will burn and have brown patches.

Pollination

Greenhouse plants may need some assistance with pollination. The pollen needs exactly the right atmospheric humidity to adhere to the female parts of the flowers and to grow down towards the ovule, and sometimes the air in the greenhouse becomes dry. The remedy is to spray the plants and the air with water, preferably in the early morning.

Sideshooting and stopping

As soon as flower trusses start to form, the plant will begin to produce shoots in the joints between stem and leaf. By nature, the tomato is a bushy plant, but allowing these shoots to grow will result in a mass of bushy foliage and a lot of under-sized fruits. Remove sideshoots by pinching them out with thumb and finger as soon as seen. This pinching out should be repeated every two or three days, for the shoots grow quickly. Early morning is the best time for the job.

Towards the end of the season, when the plant is bearing six or seven trusses of fruit, stop the plant, i.e., break off the growing tip cleanly, just above the second leaf above the top truss. The plant can then concentrate all its resources in developing and ripening the fruit on the existing trusses, rather than trying to form more leaves.

De-leafing

Removing the lower leaves of the plant will encourage it to channel its resources into fruit production and improve ventilation close to the soil. But leaves, as long as they are green, are important to a plant—they are food factories—and removal should be approached with caution. Remove only the leaves beneath the lowest truss of fruit and one or two which may be shading it. Using a sharp knife, remove the chosen leaves completely, so that a clean cut is made flush with the stem. Later on in the season, when the life of the plant can be a few weeks more at most, remove the leaves more drastically to promote ripening before the cold weather comes.

Any leaves that turn yellow should be removed completely as soon as they appear.

Feeding and watering

Tomatoes need plenty of moisture, but not a saturated soil. In borders, they should be watered heavily whenever the soil has become dry on the surface. In containers, daily watering is usually necessary, twice daily in hot weather. In greenhouses, a daily dampening in hot weather is important. This involves spraying the plants, paths, staging (benches) and walls of the greenhouse in the morning and at midday.

To produce the highest possible yield tomatoes need generous feeding. Greenhouse tomatoes will certainly benefit from regular application of nutrients. It is quite satisfactory to use a commercial tomato fertilizer, following instructions on the container. If you do want to mix your own, 2 parts sulphate of ammonia, 3 of superphosphate and 2 of sulphate of potash (all by weight) make a good, general fertilizer. Apply every seven to ten days from the time the fruits begin to swell, at the rate of about a teaspoonful sprinkled in a wide circle around each plant.

Commercial tomato fertilizers generally contain a fairly high proportion of potash, of which the plant needs liberal supplies for most of its life. Towards the end of the season, however, it will require more nitrogen to support its long stem and foliage. If the top shoot becomes thin and spindly before the plant is at the stage of pinching out, switch to a fertilizer with a higher nitrogen content and lower potash.

If, as the plant grows larger, the lower leaves start to turn yellow between the veins, the plant is probably deficient in magnesium. Correct this by spraying the plants with a solution of Epsom salts (magnesium sulphate) at the rate of 60g per 4.5 litres (2oz [¼ cup] per gallon) of water, about once a week. This condition sometimes occurs when a tomato fertilizer with a high potash content has been used too heavily. The plants absorb potash in preference to magnesium.

Harvesting and aftercare

The bottom trusses ripen first. Pick tomatoes before they are quite ripe. Remove the fruit by severing the stalk at the 'knuckle' just above the calyx. Orange-red tomatoes can complete their ripening on a windowsill within a few days, and their removal before they are fully ripe will enable the plant to divert its resources to fruit at an earlier stage of development.

When the first frosts are imminent, harvest all the tomatoes, whatever their colour. Orange, yellow and even some of the green ones will ripen indoors if each is wrapped in paper, and placed in a warm dark place, although they may take several weeks to do so. Those too small to ripen can be used for chutney.

Burn old plants, where possible, including the roots. Do not put them on the compost heap for they may well be carrying disease.

Extending the tomato season

The main advantage of taking the trouble and expense of heating a greenhouse in spring to bring on tomato plants is to have tomatoes quite early in the season, in late spring or early summer when prices are still high in the shops. There is not much point in sowing seed in autumn to try for a late winter or early spring crop, because the daylight hours are so short in late autumn and winter that seeds sown before winter will usually lie dormant for many weeks unless artificial lighting is employed, and even then extra lighting will be required for the plants.

It is possible, however, to extend the tomato season until the very end of the year by planting young plants in a greenhouse in mid-summer and providing them with heat when the frosts come.

Ring culture

Ring culture is an excellent method of growing tomatoes. It is best suited to the greenhouse, but may also be used outdoors. With this method, the plants are grown in bottomless 'rings' 23 or 25cm (9 or 10in) wide and 23cm (9in) deep, set on a base of moist aggregate (coarse sand, gravel or pebbles). The base may also be made of weathered ash or clinkers, or three parts (by volume) of gravel to one part of vermiculite. The plants develop fibrous roots which draw

nourishment from the compost in the rings, and longer roots which derive moisture from the aggregate below it.

The rings should be placed 38cm (15in) apart in rows 45cm (18in) apart. Fill each ring within 1.25cm (½in) of the top with potting compost two weeks before planting, in order to give the compost time to warm up. Water compost and aggregate two days before the plants are set out. Give an initial 1 litre (2 pts) of water to each plant through the rings, but do not water through the rings again unless the plants wilt in hot weather. Keep the aggregate wet. In about ten days, the roots should reach the aggregate. After this, water the aggregate only, keeping it permanently moist. In a hot summer you will need to give about 2 litres (3¾pts) daily for each plant, but less if the weather is cool and dull.

Make sure plants are properly supported, either with stakes put in a week after planting, or with wire and string, as for border plants.

When the fruit begins to form on the first truss, begin giving weekly liquid feeds through the rings at the rate of 1 litre (2pt) per plant. The feed should be high in potash. Half way through the season, add a 2.5cm (1in) deep top-dressing of fresh potting

Ring culture of tomatoes produces heavy crops.

compost or granulated peat. Otherwise, follow all cultivation and pruning instructions as for greenhouse tomatoes.

Bush tomatoes

Bush varieties are now available from most seed suppliers. They are hardier than ordinary tomatoes and mature more quickly, making them very useful for growing in cooler districts.

The instructions for staking, pinching out side-shoots and stopping leading shoots do not apply to bush tomatoes. Simply allow them to grow freely. They will form small bushes about 45cm (18in) high and 45cm (18in) in diameter.

Soil, manuring, watering and general culture are all the same as for ordinary tomatoes. Each plant will produce a mass of fruit, usually much smaller than the ordinary tomato but with a delicious flavour. The stems will sag under the weight of the fruit, so it is advisable to put a layer of straw or plastic over the ground beneath the bushes to keep the fruit clean.

The bush tomatoes include a number of novelties. There are plum-shaped tomatoes, pear-shaped varieties, tomatoes that grow on 'strings' like currants, and yellow bush tomatoes. Some of the smaller varieties may even be grown in pots on window sills or in window boxes.

Growing in a cold frame

Both cold frames and cloches will give a more certain chance of tomatoes developing outdoors. Because the plants can be put out considerably earlier than without protection, the tomatoes thus have a longer period of growth. Choose a slightly shaded, south-facing site, sheltered by a wall if possible, for your frame. Prepare the soil in winter by digging it over in the autumn and allow it to weather. If it is available, plenty of well-rotted farmyard manure or garden compost should be dug in at the same time, especially if the soil is light. Raise the seedlings as for growing tomatoes in a greenhouse, or buy young plants.

Put the plants in the frame in mid to late spring, or late spring to early summer for bush varieties. Two weeks before planting out, water the soil thoroughly and put the lights on to let the soil warm up. Ten days before transplanting the young plants from their 7.5cm (3in) pots, give a top dressing of three parts rotted garden compost to one part granulated peat, with 90g (3oz) of bonemeal to each bushel of the mixture.

Set the plants towards the back of the frame. Leave 45cm (18in) each way between single stem (cordon) types and train them along a cane from the back to the front of the frame. Leave the same planting distance between bush varieties. Another method of using a frame is to up-end it against a wall and use it to protect three or four tomato plants in pots or boxes.

Plants grown outdoors under frames will pollinate themselves without trouble. They will also tolerate temperatures far above 27°C (80°F) if they are given sufficient moisture. If it has been applied, farmyard manure will help to conserve moisture, but during a drought heavy daily watering is necessary, 4–5 litres (a gallon) a day is not too much per plant.

The side-shoots should be pinched out exactly as for greenhouse tomatoes, and the leading shoots should also be stopped after the formation of five trusses or so.

A very rich soil outdoors may provide all the nutrients the tomatoes require, but they are gross feeders, so if the tomato patch is not generously supplied with organic material, liquid feeding exactly as for greenhouse tomatoes will be helpful.

Growing under cloches

Prepare the soil as for frame cultivation. Then, if growing cordon tomatoes, dig a V-shaped trench, 15cm (6in) deep, 30cm (12in) wide at the top, and 15cm (6in) wide at the bottom, a week before planting. Add the same top-dressing to the bottom of the trench as used for growing under frames.

Set the plants out in mid-spring in warm areas, but a little later in cooler districts. Plant bush types 90cm (3ft) apart and cordon types 45cm (18in) apart. Extra height can be gained by standing the cloches on bricks, or you could use tall barn cloches for even more height. Remove the cloches from cordon types when the growing tips have nearly reached the tops, and thereafter treat as frame tomatoes.

Companion plants: marigolds, particularly the French variety, help to repel whiteflies, one of the most common of tomato pests, and some commercial growers have marigolds in their tomato greenhouses.

There are also plants which have a detrimental effect on each other. Growing potatoes and tomatoes near each other is to be avoided, because they are members of the same family and, therefore, attract the same problems.

Pests and diseases

Tomato moth: the green or pale brown caterpillars of the tomato moth may feed on the leaves and also the fruit, causing great damage. The moths lay their eggs in early to mid-summer, and the caterpillars are seen from mid-summer to early autumn. Caterpillars should be removed by hand and destroyed as soon as they are seen, but if the attack is very bad,

GUIDE TO TOMATO TROUBLES

Symptom	Probable cause
Irregular holes in leaves, brownish-green caterpillars	Tomato moth
Red mottling on underside of leaves	Red spider mite
Limp, curling leaves, sticky black patches; tiny white flies on undersurface	Whitefly
Small, round leaves; yellow spots, brown fur on underside	Leafmould
Dark brown blotches on leaves, stems and fruit	Potato blight
Mottled yellow and crinkled leaves	Mosaic virus
Bronze brown spots on leaves	Spotted wilt (virus)
Wilting yellow leaves; eventually whole plant wilts	Verticillium wilt
Patches of grey fur	Grey mould
Long, thin, threadlike leaves	Enation mosaic virus
Transparent spots on fruit with 'halo' around them	Water spot
Hard patches on fruit around calyx	Greenback
Yellow patches on red fruit	Blotchy ripening
Hard, sunken dark patch on fruit at clossom end	Blossom end rot
Brown rings around stem at base	Stem rot
Stunted growth; lumps or cysts on roots	Root knot eelworm, Potato eelworm

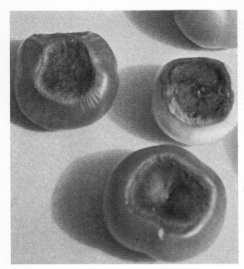

Blossom end rot of tomatoes is caused by faulty watering.

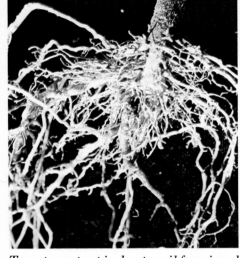

Tomato root rot is due to soil fungi and produces brown stunted roots.

Tomato split is more frequent outdoors than in the greenhouse.

spray with fenitrothion.

Eelworm: both the potato root eelworm and the root-knot eelworm can infect tomato roots, causing stunted growth, discoloured leaves and wilting plants. In severe infestations, plants will die. Plants infected by eelworm usually have tiny, cream-coloured cysts in the roots. There is no satisfactory chemical control for eelworm which is available to gardeners. Dig up and burn every scrap of the infected plants, especially the roots, and avoid growing tomatoes on the same ground for at least five years.

Stem rot (*Didymella*): this is a fungus disease which produces a corky infection that girdles the plant stems at soil level. The plants then wilt, and can be completely destroyed. Badly affected plants should be removed and burnt but, if the disease is seen early, spraying with captan may help.

Blossom end rot: this is a condition in which a round, sunken, dark brown or black patch appears on the fruit at the blossom end. It is not caused by a disease but by a severe shortage of water when the fruit is swelling. It can be prevented by regular and adequate watering.

Virus disease: a good many virus diseases for which there is no cure, can attack tomatoes. Remove any diseased plants immediately. Spotted wilt is the most serious, as it spreads rapidly and can destroy a crop. The young top leaves turn brown, and concentric rings appear on them. The plant stops growing. Thrips spread the disease, especially in the greenhouse, so control these, if seen, by spraying with malathion.

Mosaic virus shows as pale-green or yellow mottling on the leaves, together with curling and distortion. The fruits will be affected only in severe cases and will show no symptoms.

Yellow mosaic is more serious but rarely seen, with both fruit and leaves mottled with yellow patches. Diseased plants should be dug up and burned.

Enation mosaic is a commonly seen virus trouble, in which the leaves are so badly distorted as to be reduced to long, thin threads, curled and twisted, mainly near the top of the plant. Growth will stop or be slow.

Potato blight: this disease also attacks tomatoes, which are members of the same family, so take precautions by not growing potatoes and tomatoes in the same ground or too near to each other. Infected plants have dark brown to black patches on the leaves and eventually develop brown black patches on the fruit. Destroy any affected leaves as soon as you see them. Spraying with Bordeaux mixture in mid to late summer is a good preventative measure.

Verticillium wilt: a fungus disease which infects the roots of the plants, and is soil-borne. First symptoms are the wilting of the top leaves in hot weather, then the lower leaves start to turn yellow; gradually the whole plant wilts and becomes permanently limp. If the stem is cut through horizontally just above soil level, there will be a brown stain in the internal tissues. Infected plants cannot be cured, but mulching close around the stem with moist peat will encourage the plant to put out new healthy roots, which may just save it sufficiently to ripen some of the crop. Spraying the plants daily and lowering the temperature by shading or more ventilation will also help. Destroy infected plants at the end of the season, especially the roots, and sterilize the soil if tomatoes are to be grown there the following season.

Greenback: fruits have hard green patches around the stalk which never colour. The cause may be exposure to too much sun, or lack of potash.

Blotchy ripening: another functional disorder; parts of the fruit remain orange, yellow or pale green and never ripen. Insufficient potash is the cause.

Split fruit: this occurs as a result of irregular water supplies, either because a lot of water has been given after a prolonged dry period in the greenhouse, or because heavy rain follows a drought outdoors.

Red spider mite: tomatoes grown under glass are especially susceptible to red spider mite. The mites lay their eggs and feed on the underside of the leaves, producing a reddish mottled look. Fumigation of the greenhouse

The smooth-skinned greenhouse cucumbers are climbers needing support.

with azobenzene will help control the pest or spray with derris or malathion.

Whitefly: these can be one of the most troublesome tomato pests, and they can attack both greenhouse and outdoor plants. The adult flies, which look like tiny moths, lay their eggs on the undersides of leaves. The immature insects feed on the leaves, secreting honeydew which encourages sooty mould to form. The leaves look greyish and curling. As soon as you see whitefly, spray with resmethrin or malathion.

Leafmould (*Cladosporium*): this very common greenhouse disease is a fungus which causes yellow patches on the leaves. The undersides of the leaves are often covered in a brown or purple mould. The damage to foliage can be quite severe, and the flowers and fruits can also be affected. Leafmould is most likely to appear where the temperature and humidity at night are high, so maintain good ventilation without draught at such times. Keep an eye open for the disease, which tends to appear from mid-summer, and pick off infected leaves as soon as seen. If necessary, spray with benomyl. Some varieties of tomato are cladosporium resistant.

Grey mould (*Botrytis*): this fungus thrives in excessively moist atmospheres such as an unventilated greenhouse. Infected parts (leaves, stems or fruit) grow patches of grey fur, beneath which the plant tissue rots, and eventually the whole plant may die. Prevent by careful ventilation; destroy any infected plants.

Water or ghost spot: this is caused by the spores of grey mould germinating on the fruits but then drying up because of a change to warm dry conditions. It shows as small, transparent rings on the stem of the fruit and does not cause any real damage. Try not to over-water or splash water on the setting fruit.

Cucumbers

Like many other salad crops, cucumber really is at its best fresh from the garden. With a little care it is not a difficult crop to grow well, either in the greenhouse or outdoors, and the relatively high yields per plant make it well worth the effort; just three plants will produce an amount sufficient for the average family's needs.

Main types of cucumbers

There are two basic sorts of cucumbers. The first is the large, smooth-skinned type up to 38cm (15in) long. This is often called the frame, or greenhouse, cucumber because in cool temperate climates this variety needs the protection of a frame or greenhouse. These plants are grown as climbers, so the fruits can hang down. The other main type is the ridge cucumber, so called because of the old market garden practice of growing the plants on ridges outdoors. Ridge cucumbers, which include gherkins for pickling, are shorter than the greenhouse type. They are about 13cm (5in) long, with knobbly or spiny skin.

Pollination

Cucumbers produce fruit in two ways. Wild and ridge cucumbers bear separate male and female flowers on the same plant, and the female flowers need to be pollinated before fruits are produced. Greenhouse cucumbers also bear male and female flowers, but the female flowers produce fruit without pollination. These unfertilized fruits are what you should aim to produce in the greenhouse. If your greenhouse cucumbers are fertilized the fruits swell at one end, containing hard, inedible seeds. They are spoiled for exhibition use and are bitter tasting and unpleasant to eat.

Growing under glass

You can either grow your plants from seed, or buy seedlings from a reliable source. If you buy plants, choose dark green, short, stocky ones. Select ones with three or four true leaves, and the seed leaves still intact. Do not buy chilled plants from windy or exposed store areas. After buying the plants, stand them in the greenhouse for a few days in their pots. This will acclimatize them to new conditions; you can then transplant them successfully into the hot-bed.

Sow cucumber seed in compost and firm gently before watering.

Sowing

If you grow cucumbers from seed, it is best to sow them in a propagator or warm greenhouse, at an absolute minimum temperature of 15°C (60°F), but 18–25°C (65–75°F) is better. Select only plump, clean seeds and throw away any which are flat, discoloured or very small. Sow the seeds singly in clean, 6–7.5cm (2½–3in) pots, which have been filled with an appropriate seed compost (mixture) to within 1.5cm (½in) of the top of the pot. Place the seeds on edge sideways, about 1.5cm (½in) deep and lightly firm the surface. Water the compost and then cover the pots with black plastic or a sheet of glass and brown paper. Make sure the compost is thoroughly damp, because the seed casings are fairly tough. If there isn't enough moisture in the soil to penetrate the casing, the seed may not germinate. After germination, remove covering; place plants in a light position in the greenhouse. The young plants should grow rapidly and will need staking with a small, split cane. Keep the temperature at 15°C (60°F), minimum; do not let the temperature drop at night.

White roots should show on the outside of the rootball within a month of sowing; when you can see them, pot the plants on into 10–12.5cm (4½–5in) pots of an appropriate potting compost or into their final positions if you can maintain a high enough temperature.

Making a hotbed

Cucumbers require a rich, moist, well drained and aerated rooting

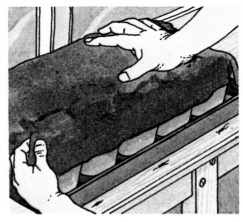

Pots should be covered, e.g. with black plastic, until germination.

medium. Greenhouse varieties are most successfully grown in beds raised above ground level. These beds should be heated; you can use hot water pipes, ducted warm air, electric heating, or heat produced by fermenting organic matter.

The base of the bed can be soil, ash, gravel, or concrete. Make sure the base is absolutely clean before building the bed.

If you plan to heat the bed by fermenting organic matter, put a layer of fresh manure in the base 45cm (18in) wide and 15cm (6in) deep. Turn this over occasionally for a few days, to allow excess nitrogen to be given off as ammonia. Another way of producing heat is to use straw. Put down a 60cm (2ft) thick layer of straw, firmed down. Sprinkle it with sulphate of ammonia and saturate the straw with water. On top of the straw or manure place a 30cm (1ft) deep and 45cm (18in) wide layer of good soil or recommended potting compost (mixture) forming it into a ridge.

Planting

When the pots are full of roots, and two to four leaves have fully expanded, nip out the growing point and plant the young cucumbers into 23cm (9in) pots. When these plants have eight or nine leaves and are 38cm (15in) high, plant them directly in the hot bed. They should be 60cm (2ft) apart, in one line down the centre of the bed.

Training

The cordon training of cucumbers is roughly similar to that of tomatoes.

Fix three wires horizontally, the top one 2.1m (7ft) high, the centre wire 1m (3ft 3in) high and the bottom wire along the surface of the bed; all three wires should be 30cm (1ft) from the outside glass of the greenhouse. Next fix a vertical string for each plant, tying it to the top, centre and base wires. Tie the leading shoot to this string at regular intervals. When the plant reaches the top wire, pinch out the growing point and tie in the lead growth. Remove all side shoots up to a height of 38cm (15in) above the base of each plant. If fruits form in the first or second leaf joints of the laterals, pinch out at two leaves beyond the fruit. If there are no fruits, stop the laterals at the second joint.

Continue tying the plant to the vertical string, stopping side shoots and removing all tendrils and male flowers until the top wire is reached. You can easily recognize male flowers, as they have no miniature cucumbers behind the petals. Continue removing the male flowers until the last fruits of the season are swelling. Remove any cucumbers which start to develop on the main stem.

Care and development

Cucumbers must be given plenty of moisture and warmth at all times, but particularly in hot weather. If you allow them to dry out at all, wilting plants, flabby fruits, pests and diseases will follow. The atmosphere in the greenhouse should be very humid. Damp down two or three times a day, always using water which is the same temperature as the greenhouse. Use a rotary sprinkler attachment to a hose, a syringe, or a watering can with a rose spray to moisten the floors, walls, staging and pots as well as the plants. When the temperature in the greenhouse rises above 24°C (75°F), you should provide ventilation, to keep the air circulating around the plants.

It is difficult to lay down hard and fast rules concerning feeding. It is generally considered best to apply a high nitrogen feed when the fruits start to swell; continue feeding twice weekly.

Top-dress the beds with a 2.5cm (1in) layer of potting compost once a month. This helps nourish the surface roots and also encourages new adventitious, or extra, roots to form at the base of the stem. The cucumber's thick coarse rooting system is particularly vulnerable to infection by fungus and bacteria, and may rot partway through the cropping season, so the continual production of healthy new roots is very important.

You must remember to remove the male flowers every four days, picking them off by hand. It is also a good idea to fix fine gauze to any ventilation openings in the greenhouse to exclude bees and flies which may enter and pollinate the female flowers. There are 'all female' varieties on the market; these produce very few male flowers and are capable of extremely high yields. 'Femspot', 'Femden' and 'Femina' are some.

Growing cucumbers in frames

Where a greenhouse is not available,

Pot on young cucumber plants when white roots are showing.

When roots have filled 12 cm (5in) pots nip out growing point.

Move to the hotbed when plants are about 45 cm (18 in) high.

Young plants can be trained up strings attached to horizontal wires.

A moist atmosphere is important so damp down frequently in hot weather.

A topdressing of potting compost will encourage the development of roots.

cucumbers can be grown successfully in a cold frame. The frame should have a stout wooden, concrete or brick base to retain warmth. Raise the seedlings as for greenhouse cultivation. In late spring place the young cucumber plants in the centre of the frame on a hotbed, as described earlier. If you have no hotbeds, delay planting until early summer. Keep the frame closed, except for occasional ventilation on warm days, but when the weather is very warm leave the frame light off all day. Remember to replace it at night, when the temperature drops.

Pinch out the growing tips when four or five leaves have formed on each plant. Shortly afterwards, shoots will be produced in the axils (joints) of these leaves. Select the four strongest shoots and train one towards each corner of the frame. Carry out watering, feeding, and pinching out side shoots as described above. As the fruits develop, place a sheet of glass or piece of slate under the fruits, to keep them from becoming soiled or discoloured. Remember to remove any male flowers. Shade the plants from strong sunlight to prevent scorching.

Harvesting

Greenhouse cucumbers will start to crop in late spring or early summer, and fruits should be cut when about 30–37cm (1–1ft 3in) long. Cropping should continue until autumn. Ridge cucumbers sown under cloches will begin to crop in late summer, or early autumn if they have been sown in the open ground. Outdoor cropping will continue until the first frosts, when the plants will be killed. Harvest the cucumbers when they are young and crisp; old fruits go to seed and if left on the plant cause further fruit production to cease. If you have a bumper crop, pickle them if they are the ridge variety, or give the extra cucumbers to friends or neighbours. Cucumbers are at their best when freshly picked; they do not store well.

Pests and diseases

The warm, moist conditions in which cucumbers flourish provide the perfect environment for bacterial and

GUIDE TO CUCUMBER TROUBLES

Symptoms	Probable cause
Leaves turn yellow; silky webs on plants	Red spider mite
Small green insects; leaves turn yellow	Greenfly
Clouds of minute insects	Whitefly
Holes in stems of young plants, silvery slime	Slugs
Holes in leaves and surface of young fruit, grey, hard shelled creatures	Woodlice
Leaves discoloured, plant collapses	Root knot eelworm
Grey fluffy growth on stems, fruit and leaves	Botrytis
Leaves wilt, stem becomes dark, plant dies	Collar rot
Leaves mottled yellow; plant wilts, dies	Mosaic virus
Leaves turn yellow from base upwards	Verticillium wilt
Sunken oozing spots on fruit	Gummosis
Wet, dark wounds on stems, leaves and fruit	Sclerotinia disease

Roots infected with collar rot.

A severe attack of botrytis.

Whitefly on the underside of leaves.

Cucumber mosaic virus mottling.

fungal infections. Since many of these are encouraged by improper watering and ventilating, make sure you are cultivating the plants properly. Be on the lookout for any sign of infection and act quickly to control it, because disease will spread rapidly in close greenhouse or frame conditions. When you use an insecticide on cucumbers, be sure to choose one that will not damage the plants; the *Cucurbitaceae* family is sensitive to some chemical sprays.

Red spider mite: this pest causes the leaves to turn yellow; if severely in-

fected, the plant will become bronze coloured, wilt and collapse. Another sign of red spider mite is the appearance of silky webs around the leaves and stems. The best preventative action is to maintain damp conditions in the greenhouse or outdoors. The best control is to spray the infected plants with derris or soft soap.

Greenfly: these small green insects are usually found in colonies on or near the growing points and under the leaves, which may turn yellowy grey and wither. Control greenfly by smokes or sprays of malathion or nicotine. Use the nicotine with care, as overuse may blanch the leaves; if this happens, cut off the bleached leaves immediately and spray with a nicotine soap wash.

Whitefly: if, when you disturb the leaves of cucumber plants, clouds of minute insects appear, then the plants are infested with whitefly. These insects are very destructive and weakening; they feed chiefly on the sap and excrete honeydew which encourages the growth of sooty mould. Spray with malathion as soon as whiteflies are seen.

Slugs: slug damage can usually be spotted by holes in the stems of young plants and the presence of silvery slime trains. Commercial pellets are the most effective control.

Woodlice: these are grey, minute armadillo-shaped creatures which roll up into small balls when touched. They eat holes in the leaves and may also attack the surface of young fruits. Woodlice are most likely to occur in old greenhouses or frames; spray or dust around the roots of infected plants with BHC (HCH).

Root knot eelworm: plants indoors and outdoors may be attacked by these microscopic pests which invade the roots. Leaves may become discoloured; in bad cases the whole plant may collapse. Although some plants may survive mild infections, it is best to dig up and burn any diseased plant. There is no absolutely effective control, but if one plant is infected, it is a good idea to treat the soil with a sterilant such as formaldehyde before growing susceptible crops in the same place.

Botrytis: this grey fluffy growth on the stems, fruits, and leaves is best controlled by benomyl sprays. Badly infected plants should be removed and burned, as they will never crop well.

Collar rot: this usually affects greenhouse cucumbers which are growing in badly drained soil or have been over-watered. The plants are attacked by soil-borne organisms at or slightly above ground level. The leaves wilt, the stems become dark and the plants die. Preventive measures of raised beds, well-aerated soil, and good hygiene are useful. Plants which are not too badly damaged

may be saved by removing all decaying tissue and dusting the infected areas with captan. Then raise the level of the soil 3.5cm (1½in) around the stem to encourage the growth of new adventitious roots. In 10 days top-dress again. Pull out and destroy badly infected plants; treat the soil around adjacent plants with benomyl or captan.

Mosaic virus: the leaves of plants infected with mosaic virus become yellow and mottled; the whole plant then rapidly wilts, shrivels up and dies. As there is no effective control for the virus, and it is carried by greenfly, the best prevention is to control greenfly.

Verticillium wilt: this soil-borne fungus causes the leaves to turn yellow from the base upwards. The

disease is more liable to occur in cold, wet conditions. It usually attacks the roots of young plants; older plants are vulnerable if they have open wounds. Eventually the diseased plants wilt, and should be dug up and burned. Apply Cheshunt compound to the soil before replanting.

Gummopsis of cucumber: this fungus disease affects plants grown in a greenhouse or frame; it spreads quickly in cold, wet conditions. Infected fruits develop sunken spots which ooze a gummy liquid; this spot is eventually covered with dark spores. Occasionally small spots appear on the stems or leaves. Keeping

Greenhouse cucumbers should be harvested when young and fresh.

the greenhouse or frame warm and well ventilated is a good preventive measure. Control gummosis by spraying with zineb or captan; destroy all diseased fruits. Disinfect the greenhouse or frame before replanting.

Sclerotinia disease: wet, dark wounds appear on the stem, leaves and fruits, followed by fluffy, white growths with black central areas. Dig up and burn any infected plants.

Anthracnose: the leaves will have small pale patches which quickly turn brown and grow bigger until the whole leaf dies; stems are sometimes affected. Remove and destroy badly infected plants. Spray the remaining plants with 1 part lime sulphur to 60 parts water with a spreading agent. Make sure that the greenhouse is well ventilated, and spray it with formalin when empty.

Lettuce

This vegetable (*Lactuca* species and varieties) is the basic ingredient of most salads and a continuous supply is important. By full use of the greenhouse, cold frames and cloches, the good gardener is able to raise lettuces for at least six months of the year.

The production of winter and early spring lettuces is not easy and these crops are a challenge to the gardener.

Lettuces fall into three groups— cabbage, cos and loose-leaf. The cabbage kinds are subdivided into crispheads and butterheads. Those sold by the greengrocer are almost always butterheads because crispheads do not travel well and wilt rather quickly after harvesting. The cos varieties have long, boat-shaped, very crisp leaves and they are preferred by many for their fine flavour. Loose-leaf lettuces are very popular in the United States, although one American variety, 'Salad Bowl', is liked by gardeners everywhere.

Any check to steady growth is liable to result in rather poor lettuces. Water is very important, but the soil must be sufficiently porous to allow for good drainage.

The first sowings may be made under glass in January or February and a greenhouse temperature of 13–16°C (55–60°F) is suitable. Sow thinly and not deeply in shallow trays and prick off into deeper ones as soon as possible after germination, allowing each seedling 5 sq cm (2 sq in) of space. Harden off in the cold frame in

late March and plant out on a mild day in April. Plant with a ball of the compost mixture adhering to the roots at 30cm (12in) apart in the row. If cloches are available, the small plants may be set out beneath them in late March.

A sowing made in late July provides lettuces in November and December but here again, the weather plays an important part. The rows need cloche protection from October onwards. For early spring supplies, sow in the cold frame in September and, subsequently, replant the seedlings in the greenhouse or in frames. Alternatively, sow in the greenhouse in early October and transplant when the plants have four leaves. Deep planting at any time is unwise. It is particularly dangerous where lettuces are to be over-wintered. Overcrowding must also be avoided and correct ventilation is very important.

Among the very many varieties on offer, the following may be relied upon for worthwhile crops.

For early sowings under glass: 'May

Left: crisphead lettuce.
Right: loose-leaf lettuce.

Queen' (syn. 'May King').
For sowing under glass for early spring cutting: 'May Queen', 'Cheshunt Early Giant', 'Kordaat', 'Kloek'.

Other vegetables

In addition to those already mentioned, other vegetables and salad crops well worth growing in a cool greenhouse are mustard and cress, radishes and aubergines (egg plants). Rhubarb and seakale can also be forced under the greenhouse staging in complete darkness.

Aubergine (Egg plant)

This plant comes from tropical or semi-tropical climates. It is grown in greenhouses in cooler climates, or it may be grown in a frame from May onwards and even outside in a very sheltered position in warmer areas. The fruits vary in size and shape from roundish to sausage-shaped and are usually a very deep purple, but there are white varieties. Botanically it is known as *Solanum melongena ovigerum*. It makes a small bush 60–90cm (2–3ft) high and has blue flowers.

Sow the seeds in a heated house, about 18°C (65°F), in January, February or March in a suitable seed compost (mixture). Prick out the seedlings as soon as possible into 5½cm (2½in) pots and pot on, finally into 18cm (7in) pots using a suitable potting compost (mixture). Water well and pinch out the tips to encourage bushiness when the plants are 15cm (6in) high. Restrict the fruits to four to six per plant and feed the plants with weak liquid manure or a balanced fertilizer at regular intervals. Gather the fruits when slightly soft.

Peppers

Red and green peppers, or capsicums, need warm, moist conditions. Seed is sown in early March under glass in a suitable compost (mixture), in a temperature of 16°C (60°F). The final potting should be in 18cm (7in) pots, or plants may be grown in the greenhouse border. Feed with nitrogenous fertilizer and provide support for the

Peppers will crop well in warm, moist conditions if well fertilized.

taste. The plants are generally raised from cuttings taken from growing plants in the autumn. The plants are grown for their tender young shoots. Unless blanched, they are bitter and unpalatable. For the earliest crop of blanched shoots, lift a few plants in November and cut off the thongy side growths for the preparation of cuttings for new plants for spring planting. Plant the strong main roots and crowns closely together in large clay pots, using old potting soil as the compost. Water moderately and stand the pots in a dark, heated place. If blanching is carried out in the garden shed, cover the window, if beneath the greenhouse staging, drape a sheet of black polythene over and around the pots to exclude light. Further roots may be dug and forced in the same way on and off between November and February. A temperature of between 16–24°C (60–75°F) should be maintained.

Frames and cloches (Hotkaps)

As far as vegetables are concerned, the garden frame and cloche are considered to be as useful as the greenhouse.

Vegetables for frame cultivation

Lettuce An ideal crop for frames. With careful management, heads for cutting can be grown all year round. The use of suitable varieties is most essential, particularly for winter work. For cutting in March and early April, seed should be sown in late October and the seedlings planted 30cm (12in) apart each way in December. The varieties 'May King', 'Early French Frame' and 'Attractie' are suitable for unheated frames. For heated frames use 'Cheshunt Early Giant'.

Cold frame lettuces in winter need ample protection against frost and during dull, wet weather, ventilation must be provided to prevent mildew. It is a wise precaution to dust with sulphur. Do not over water; the ideal is to apply only sufficient to prevent the soil drying out. Lettuces are

plants. Plants may also be grown out of doors in a sunny border. They should be raised in the greenhouse and planted out in June. Give them plenty of water and spray them overhead in dry weather. The large types are peppers or capsicums, the small ones chillies.

Rhubarb

Rhubarb can be forced in the shed or greenhouse. The roots should be lifted as and when required and exposed to frost for a few days. Plant the frosted roots closely together in boxes of soil or beneath the greenhouse staging. Water them well and exclude light by draping black polythene sheeting or

Forced rhubarb does not have the rich colour of that grown outdoors.

sacking over and around the roots. At a temperature of between 16°-21°C (60–70°F), sticks will be ready for use within a month or so. In unheated sheds and greenhouses, growth will be considerably slower and the roots may need watering occasionally. Use a fine rose on the can when doing so. Discard all roots after they have been forced in this way.

Sea kale

This plant (which is known botanically as *Crambe maritima*) is much appreciated by those who know its

most welcome in the autumn and a sowing made in mid-August will provide mature hearts from October onwards. A suitable variety is 'Attractie'.

To maintain regular supplies during the early summer and onwards, frequent small sowings will be necessary. Sow approximately once every three weeks to maintain continuity. The first sowing in the spring should be in late February or early March. 'Early French Frame', 'Market Favourite' and 'May King' are three reliable varieties. For the early summer and main summer sowings, use varieties such as 'Holborn Standard', 'Continuity' and 'Perpetual'.

Carrots When young and tender, carrots possess an individual flavour and if these are grown as an early crop in the frame, a worthwhile supply can be easily produced. An early, forced crop is the best and seed should be sown broadcast and as thinly as possible. It is essential that the soil be broken down as fine as possible before sowings. Suitable sowing times are January and February. Cover seed lightly and keep the soil moist. Lights must go on the frames immediately after sowing. Pickings should start in late May and early June. Suitable varieties are 'Amsterdam Forcing' and 'Early Nantes'. The former is particularly suitable for unheated frames. Weeds must be removed regularly and as soon as they are noticed. Ventilation is also important and should be increased gradually as the season advances.

Turnips Turnips should be sown in late February or mid March for sweet roots in late May or early June, using seed of the variety 'Early White Milan'. Sow in shallow drills, spacing these 25cm (10in) apart. Early thinning of seedlings is essential so that there is room for the round roots to develop. Usually this variety is ready for pulling when the roots are about 6cm (2.5in) in dia-

Seakale can be forced in the greenhouse for the tender young shoots.

meter. The soil must be kept moist to encourage rapid swelling of the roots. Lights can be removed after mid-April but a watch must be kept for late frosts.

Radish The radish is another good crop for frames as it matures rapidly, given good growing conditions. Large crops are not required at any one time so it is better to use radishes as a catch crop between other slow-growing ones. Make frequent sowings at three-week intervals, if necessary starting in early February. The crop should be ready for gathering from late March onwards. Shallow drills should be taken out for the seed between other crop rows and the seed sown very thinly. Water frequently, maintaining a steady supply, and ventilate according to weather conditions.

Tomatoes Frames can be very useful to gardeners in exposed and cold regions with late springs. Where tomatoes can be grown in a frame, the main purpose being to give important early protection so that

Above: turnips are easy to grow and both tops and roots are edible.
Below: radishes can be grown in frames from late winter on.

sturdy, well-established plants are produced. If a heated frame is available it will be possible to raise the plants from seed sown in mid-March in pans or pots.

For more explicit cultivation instructions see pages 60-67.

Cucumbers Frame or greenhouse types are suitable and are well worth growing, especially if there is no greenhouse available. Full growing instructions are given on pages 67-72.

Melons Melons do best in hot summers, nevertheless this is a crop which is worth a trial, especially in warmer gardens. If there are no facilities for raising plants in heat in early May, they should be purchased from a reliable nursery or garden shop. Soil preparations are exactly the same as for cucumbers. Plant out in mid-May or early June in an unheated frame.

Training and watering are as for cucumbers except that only 3 to 4 fruits should be allowed per plant if reasonable sized ones are to be expected. Unlike the cucumbers, hand pollination must be carried out with a small brush, transferring dry pollen from a male flower to a female flower. The latter is easily recognized by the tiny fruit immediately behind the base of the petals. In order to ensure dry pollen, the atmosphere of the frame should be kept dry when

or planting takes place, the ground will be warmed slightly and will be maintained in a suitable condition despite bad weather.

Beetroot (Beet) For early supplies, a late February sowing is made in warmer areas. For general sowings March is a suitable month. Small or large cloches are used depending on the number of rows required. Sow a single row under small cloches, three rows under larger ones, spacing these 15cm (6in) apart. All seed is sown as thinly as possible, about 2.5cm (1in) deep. Early thinning is necessary when seedlings can be handled easily. A later thinning is advised when roots the size of a golf ball are lifted. These are excellent for salads. Plants left in the rows are allowed to mature. 'Detroit Selected' and 'Crimson Ball' are suitable.

Broad beans Seed is sown in mid-November in cooler areas and late January in warmer. Tall cloches (hotkaps), or additional height provided by special adaptors, are necessary in late spring for frost pro-

several flowers have formed.

When fruits have set and are swelling well, place a piece of board under each one to prevent marking and slug damage. A little slug bait should be placed in the corners of the frame. Feed as for cucumbers and topdress with soil whenever necessary.

Melons are ripe when a heavy odour or perfume is noticed and when the area immediately around the stalk begins to crack. The area around the flower end also becomes soft. Varieties to use are 'Dutch Net' or 'Tiger'. Both are cantaloupe melons with attractive orange flesh.

Marrows and squash Squash and marrows are usually grown in the open garden, but an earlier planting and cropping season can be achieved if a frame can be spared. Culture is the same as for cucumbers. The best type to grow is the bush, which requires no special training.

Growing vegetables under cloches (Hotkaps)

A week before sowing or planting apply a well-balanced general fertilizer at the rate of 75g (3oz) per sq m (sq yd). This is raked in thoroughly and raking action will also break the soil down ready for sowing or planting. If cloches are placed over the prepared strips a week before sowing

Above: as radishes soon spoil, plant small quantities in succession.
Below: for early beetroot, plant in late winter under cloches (Hotkaps).

tection to tall plants. Sow a double row in a 7.5cm (3in) deep, flat bottom drill which is 20cm (8in) wide. Space the seeds 20cm (8in) apart in staggered fashion. Two suitable varieties are 'Aquadulce' and 'Early Long Pod'.

Dwarf beans Three sowings can be made: mid-March in warm areas, early April in cooler and, for a late crop to be picked approximately in October, a July sowing can be made. For all sowings the variety 'Lightning' is ideal. Seed is sown under the larger cloches in a double row in a flat 15cm (6in) wide trench, 5cm (2in) deep. Stagger seeds 20cm (8in) apart. If drying beans are required, haricots should be sown in mid-April in all districts as above. A good variety to use is 'Comtesse du Chambourd'.

Runner beans In warm areas seed is sown in mid-March and in late April in cooler. Large barn cloches are used making a double row sowing with the rows 23cm (9in) apart. Seeds are placed 5cm (2in) deep and 20-25cm (8-10in) apart. As the plants are staked individually later on, the seeds are not staggered, but placed opposite each other. 'Streamline' and 'Kelvedon Wonder' are reliable.

Brussels sprouts Cloches are used solely as seed raisers to give plants a long growing period after an early start. Seed is sown thinly in shallow drills under one or more cloches. Young plants are pricked out later into another seed bed and finally planted 75cm (2.5ft) apart each way in their permanent quarters. In the warmer areas a sowing can be made in late January using varieties such as 'Cambridge No. 1', for early pickings, and 'Cambridge No. 5' for late crops. As soon as conditions allow in cooler areas a sowing can be made in February using 'Cambridge No. 1' or 'The Wroxton'.

Carrots Five sowings are made according to district. In warm areas early January will provide the first pickings if a variety such as 'Primo' is used. The earliest possible sowing date in cooler areas is mid to late February with a variety such as 'Early Nantes'. Gardeners in warmer areas can make another sowing in February for a prolonged supply of

the early 'Primo'. For a late November supply of carrots in cooler areas, an August sowing of 'Primo' is advised. The seedlings must be cloched in September before first frosts threaten. Late crops for gardeners in warmer areas are obtained if a September to October sowing is made using the varieties 'Early Nantes' or 'Primo'. Large cloches should be used, and four or five rows can be accommodated. Thin sowing

Dwarf beans are compact plants which give a high yield.

is necessary in 6mm (¼in) deep drills spaced 10-13cm (4-5in) apart.

Cauliflowers Three sowings can be made, using a cloche or two as a seed raiser. Early September for cooler areas and late September for warmer areas are the first sowing dates for early crops. Large cloches should be used so that three drills can be made.

78

Sow thinly and thin later to 5cm (2in) apart. Plant out finally in March and April 60cm (2ft) apart each way. If very large cloches are available, some plants can be covered to maturity. A suitable variety for these sowings is 'All The Year Round'. In warmer areas a further sowing can be made in January and late in February for cooler districts. In both instances plants are raised under a few cloches and finally planted out in outdoor beds. The same variety can be used.

Cucumbers Frame and ridge types can be used. The former is hardier and cloche protection is necessary during early stages of growth only. Plants can be purchased and set out under cloches in late April or seed can be raised under a cloche in early April in warmer areas and late April or early May in cooler. Whichever method is adopted, plants are finally planted out 90cm (3ft) apart in a single row. For each plant a special site should be prepared, taking out a hole 30cm (1ft) square and half filling it with old manure or composted vegetable waste. The remainder of the hole should be filled up with good soil, mixed with a little

horticultural peat.

Plants are trained in a special way. When the fourth true leaf has formed, the growing point of the plant is removed. Several lateral growths should form and the two strongest are selected; the others

Sowing cauliflowers under cloches can give a succession of crops.

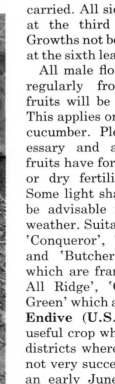

Leave flowers on ridge cucumbers; pollination is essential to get fruit.

removed. These two are trained to run along the direction of the cloche row, one on either side of the plant. When these growths have produced six leaves, they are stopped. Side growths should form on the laterals and it is on these that the fruit is carried. All side growths are stopped at the third leaf beyond a fruit. Growths not bearing fruit are stopped at the sixth leaf.

All male flowers must be removed regularly from plants, otherwise fruits will be bitter and malformed. This applies only to the frame type of cucumber. Plenty of water is necessary and as soon as the first fruits have formed, weak liquid feeds or dry fertilizer should be given. Some light shading of the glass may be advisable in very warm, bright weather. Suitable varieties to use are 'Conqueror', 'Improved Telegraph', and 'Butcher's Disease Resisting' which are frame types, and 'Best of All Ridge', 'Greenline' and 'Long Green' which are ridge cucumbers.

Endive (U.S. Chicory) This is a useful crop which replaces lettuce in districts where lettuce cultivation is not very successful. In warmer areas an early June sowing is ideal and later that month in cooler gardens. Two rows are sown thinly under large barn cloches, spacing the rows 30cm

(12in) apart and sowing the seed 12mm (½in) deep. Seedlings are thinned eventually to 30cm (1ft) apart. The crop is covered in early September to protect from early frosts. The plants must be blanched or whitened. This is easily done if a flat object such as an inverted plate or saucer is placed over the centre of each plant. In about six weeks the leaves will have blanched sufficiently. The best variety is 'Round-leaved Batavian'.

Lettuce Late September is the sowing time in all districts for lettuce which will be ready for cutting from approximately March to May. Large barn cloches are used to accommodate three rows of seeds. Sow thinly and thin in November 25cm (10in) apart. Cloches remain over until April or late May in colder districts. Suitable varieties are 'Attraction' and 'May King'.

In late January a further sowing can be made in warm areas. These lettuces should be ready for cutting in June. Similar growing techniques are required except that the original sowing must be even thinner to minimize thinning or transplanting checks. 'May King' and 'Perpetual'

For early spring lettuces, sow in autumn and give cloche protection.

are good varieties.

Gardeners in cooler areas should make a sowing in late March. When large enough to handle, thin plants to 30cm (1ft) apart. Cloches can be removed in early June when frost danger has passed. 'Trocadero Improved', 'Wonderful' and 'Buttercrunch' are ideal varieties.

For a late November supply of lettuce in cooler areas a sowing can be made in late July. Thin plants to at least 30cm (1ft) apart to allow plenty of air to circulate round plants in early September. 'May King', 'Market Favourite' and 'Attraction' can be recommended.

The most suitable time to sow cos lettuce in all districts is March. Cover immediately with cloches which are removed in early June. Two rows can be sown under a large barn cloche. Seedlings must be thinned to 30cm (1ft) apart. A good variety to sow is 'Giant White'.

Marrow and squash Sow in late April in cooler areas and late March in warmer. Culture is similar to that required for cucumbers except that

the compact bush types are the best to grow. These require no stopping or training. To ensure a good set of fruit, hand pollination is advisable. The cloches are kept over the plants until early June. Suitable varieties are 'Tender and True', 'Green or White Bush' and 'Courgette'.

Peas For first sowings in cooler areas, early October is the best month and in warmer sowings are carried out in November. The next sowing in the warmer areas is January and in all districts sow again in March.

Sow in 20cm (8in) wide flat drills, 5cm (2in) deep. The seed is scattered in staggered formation 5-7. 5cm (2-3in) apart each way in three rows. The cloches remain over the plants from early sowings until the foliage is practically touching the roof glass. The peas can be decloched in early April when seed is sown in March. Early training with small twigs or brushwood is essential for good growth. Plenty of water is required once the plants are well established from the spring onwards. Suitable varieties are 'Meteor' for the October or November sowings, 'Kelvedon Wonder' for January sowings and 'Laxton's Superb' for the March sowings.

Potatoes Spring supplies of new potatoes can be produced by planting them in warm frames in mid-winter, either directly in the soil or in pots, but few gardeners have this much frame accommodation. Half bury each upright set in a 20cm (8int pot about a third full, and earth them up as they grow. Potatoes can be successfully grown in pots under glass. Fill 20cm (8in) pots with a good quality compost and plant one sprouted tuber in each pot. If you have a heated greenhouse, plant the tubers in late winter and the potatoes will be ready in late spring. If you have an unheated greenhouse or cold frame, expect potatoes in early summer from an early spring planting.

Radish This crop (like the lettuce and early carrots), is an ideal catch crop or intercrop. Out of season sowings are more valuable for cloche work and in warm areas sowings are made in late September and frequently from then onwards until late

March. For gardeners in cooler areas, September and October are suitable months for late work and the end of February until late April for the early spring. Seed is sown thinly in shallow drills when used as a catch crop or broad cast under one or two cloches. The smaller cloches are particularly suitable for the latter purpose. Suitable varieties are 'French Breakfast' and 'Scarlet Globe'.

Sweet corn This is one crop in particular which is grown more easily in temperate areas with the aid of cloches. In cooler areas a sowing can be made in early May, and in warmer areas in the second or third week in April. Seed is sown *in situ* or where the plants are to grow to maturity. Sow seed 25cm (10in) apart in double rows spaced 30cm (1ft) apart. Two seeds per station are sown, removing the weakest seedling later on. This crop should not be transplanted.

When the foliage reaches the roof the crop can be decloched. Plenty of water is essential during hot, dry weather. There is no need to remove sidegrowths. A little soil should be drawn up on either side of the rows when the plants are about 1m (3ft) high. This helps to anchor them and is an essential part of their culture in exposed districts. The cobs are ripe when the grain inside the cobs exudes a milky fluid as they are squeezed with the finger nails. Suitable varieties are 'Fogwill's Extra Early', 'Golden Bantam' and 'Canada Crop'.

Tomatoes Outdoor tomatoes are usually a rather chancy crop in temperate zones as a long spell of good weather is needed to get the bulk of the fruit ripened before frosts cut the plants down. Cloches have an invaluable part to play in the successful culture of this plant. They can either give the plants vital early protection so that they become estab-

lished quickly or they can provide continuous protection which will produce crops nearly as early as glasshouse ones. Gardeners will welcome this type of protection in districts which are much colder.

The site for the crop should be prepared thoroughly by deep cultivation. Separate positions can be prepared for each plant as for cucumbers and marrows. A general fertilizer is applied a few days before planting at the rate of 75g (3oz) per sq m (sq yd). The plants are best purchased from a reliable source. Good plants are short jointed and deep green in colour. The plants should be set out 60cm (2ft) apart in the row, with 1m (3ft) between each row.

Two shapes of tomato plant can be grown, the cordon and the bush. Where it is intended to grow entirely under cloches, the bush type is ideal. As soon as the plants have been set out they should be staked and tied securely. All sideshoots must be removed from cordon plants as soon as they are noticed. In early June, it will be safe enough in all districts to remove the cloches entirely except where it is intended to grow to maturity under them. Plenty of water must be given, especially when the first flower trusses have set. Dry or weak liquid feeds will be required to encourage heavy trusses of fruit.

When cordon plants have produced four trusses, they should be stopped. This is done by removing the centre or growing point of the plants. Bush tomatoes require no stopping or sideshooting. Several varieties can be grown out of doors. Of the cordons, 'Outdoor Girl' and 'Essex Wonder' are excellent. There are several very good bush varieties. These include 'Amateur Improved', 'Atom' and 'Dwarf Cloche'. The latter two varieties are exceptionally useful as they grow to a height and spread of only 38cm (15in).

Whichever method suits your garden—greenhouse, frame or cloche—growing vegetables under glass will always give satisfaction as well as the pleasure of really fresh produce.

Cloches in pairs on end can be used to protect young tomato plants.

Fruit under glass

While bananas and pineapples require so much heat that they are mostly outside the range of the ordinary amateur gardener, a number of hardier fruits can be obtained earlier with the aid of glass protection.

Some heat is necessary. The blossom and newly-set fruitlets of all so-called hardy fruits are vulnerable to frost. In an unheated greenhouse sun-heat is stored up during the daytime so that the average temperature is well above that prevailing outside. Further, the occupants of such a house are not exposed to chilling, growth-inhibiting winds, and these two factors result in earlier blossoming. This, of course, increases the risk of frost coinciding with flowering. Just sufficient heating, therefore, must be available to keep the temperature above 0°C (32°F) during the coldest weather.

Greater heat than this is not really necessary but if you aspire to eating ripe strawberries in April and early May some regular heating will be required.

Any hardy fruits can be grown under glass but those generally considered the most rewarding are peaches, nectarines, figs and grapes. Strawberries are accommodating because they occupy the house for three or four months only, leaving the space available for other purposes during the remainder of the year. Further, you can force strawberries one year, if you wish, and not the next, but once a fruit or a vine is planted, it is 'there for good'. Melons are another possibility for the greenhouse-owner and these are in a category on their own.

Where space is at a premium, fruit trees may also be grown under glass in pots. This restricts root action so that the trees remain small. Pot-grown specimens of apples, cherries, figs, peaches and nectarines, pears, plums and greengages may be obtained for this purpose from specialist nurseries.

Peaches and nectarines

Both these fruits are treated in the same way, the latter simply being a smooth-skinned form of peach. They are usually grown as fans and are most easily accommodated against the back wall of a lean-to house, but they may also be trained on wires fixed 60cm (2ft) away from the glass or on a trellis arranged across the house.

Although plenty of water will be required in the growing season, drainage must be impeccable. If necessary, therefore, the border should be excavated to a depth of about 90cm (3ft) and either field-drain pipes laid, or a foot depth of rubble put in. A layer of turves (sods) laid grass-side down, will prevent the soil above from clogging the drainage. The peach tree will need a depth of 45–60cm (18–24in) for its roots but this soil should not be too rich or excessive growth will be encouraged in the early years at the expense of fruiting.

For a path, wooden duck-boarding is preferable to concrete so that moisture can penetrate and the roots be free to extend.

Trees should be planted in the usual way and the young growths tied to canes which in their turn, are tied to wires. Training and pruning follow similar lines as for outdoor trees, but remember that in the greenhouse the trees will receive only the water you give them. The border will need to be flooded in January to start growth; and frequent watering will be necessary when growth becomes active. Syringeing is also necessary, once or twice daily, from bud break until the fruit begins to colour. This syringeing may be quite forceful, to discourage pests. While the flowers are open, the syringeing should be reduced to once a day, around midday, to encourage pollination.

In January the house ventilators should be closed early in the afternoon to trap the sun's warmth, the temperature being maintained as near to 4°C (40°F) as manipulation of the ventilators can secure. In February the temperature may be allowed to rise to around 10°C (50°F) but, should very cold weather prevail during the blossom period and immediately after, some heating will be necessary to keep the temperature at least above freezing point.

Pollination is the difficulty with fruits under glass because the insects which usually perform the service for us are not present. A hive of bees may be stood in the greenhouse but for most gardeners this is impossible and resort should be made to hand-fertilization of the blossom, transferring the pollen about midday with a rabbit's tail (if you can get one), a camel's hair brush or a small piece of cotton wool tied to the end of a stick. Do this before syringeing as an additional aid.

In March, the temperature may rise to 13–16°C (65–60°F); but when outside temperatures begin to exceed this try to keep the atmosphere in the house buoyant by adequate damping down and ample ventilation. From May on some light shading should be provided—with blinds or strips of plastic netting shading material or by spraying or painting the roof glass with a commercial shading preparation.

Thinning of the fruit should be carried out, as with the outdoor crop, in easy stages. If large fruits are wanted, the final allowance of space should be about 30sq cm (12sq in) per peach and 23sq cm (9sq in) for each nectarine, but for average size, thinning may be less drastic, allowing from 23 to 15sq cm (9 to 6sq in) per fruit.

As ripening begins, all syringeing must stop and more air should be given. Foliage which shades the fruit should be tied back temporarily.

Once the peach crop has been gathered, spray as forcefully as you can and ventilate as freely as possible to assist the ripening of the new wood. Continue to water the border regularly. Ventilators should be left open, night and day, until January when growth is to be restarted. Untying and pruning may be done early in the autumn.

If spraying with tar-oil is considered necessary to control aphids and scale insects, this may be done as soon as it is certain that the tree concerned is quite dormant.

Feeding is seldom necessary in the first year or two as it may result in growth rather than fruit. Some food, however, will be needed once heavy crops are being carried. A mixture of 2 parts of sulphate of ammonia, 2 parts of superphosphate and 1 part of sulphate of potash, all parts by weight, should be scattered over the border at the rate of 150g per 2sq m (5oz per 2sq yd), and lightly raked in and then watered. In March, put down a mulch of rotted stable manure or garden compost. If the burden of fruit bearing appears to be too great and fresh growth is being made only slowly, an extra fillip can be given after storing, in the form of liquid manure or dried blood applied at the rate of 125g per sq m (4oz per sq yd) of border.

Peaches under glass are liable to the same pests and diseases as those in the open, although peach leaf curl is usually less troublesome and red spider mite very much more so. The following varieties, given in order of ripening, are suitable for greenhouse cultivation, those marked with an asterisk being the most reliable:

Peaches: 'Duke of York'*, 'Waterloo', 'Peregrine'*, 'Royal George', 'Dymond'*, 'Bellegarde'.
Nectarines: 'Early Rivers', 'Lord Napier'*, 'Pineapple'.

Figs

Whereas figs in the open will only ripen one crop of fruit a year, those in a heated greenhouse can ripen two. With sufficient heat it is even possible to secure three crops a year, but this is a heavy drain on the strength of the tree and expensive in fuel consumption as it is necessary to start growth in mid-winter with a temperature of 18–20°C (65–70°F), gradually rising to 27°C (80°F).

The fig is most conveniently trained as a fan against the wall of a lean-to house. The soil in the border should not be rich as this would encourage growth at the expense of fruit—a very average loam will serve. Indeed, to keep growth within the confines of even a fair-sized greenhouse it is advisable to restrict the roots, doing this by making up the border inside a concrete 'box'. Wooden shuttering should be used to make a bottomless box, 120cm long x 60cm wide and 60cm deep (4ft x 2ft and 2ft deep). When the concrete has set hard, dig out a little soil from the bottom and replace with a layer of

broken brick or stone, well rammed in place, so that free drainage is possible but the formation of taproots discouraged.

Fill this box with light soil, adding sand or brick or mortar rubble if the natural soil in the garden is not sandy or gravelly. Do not add manure.

Turn on the heat to start growth in early spring with a temperature around 13–16°C (55–60°F). The border will need flooding at the start of the season and plenty of water will be required when the tree is in full growth. It helps growth (and deters red spider mites) to damp down the path and syringe the foliage regularly from bud break until the autumn, withholding the spray while the fruit is ripening.

When the second crop has been picked, probably in September, gradually cut down the water supply and, when all the leaves have dropped, let the tree rest, with free ventilation, no heat and the minimum amount of moisture. Close the house during frost and give a little warmth only when conditions are severe and the temperature inside the

house is likely to fall below freezing point.

Pruning and disbudding follow similar lines as for outdoor figs but it should be remembered that the second (autumn) crop is borne on the new wood made that spring and summer. Embryo figs on the tips of the new growths will give the next season's spring crop. Therefore, there must be no summer pinching of new shoots.

As with peaches, red spider mites may be a nuisance on figs under glass, particularly if conditions have been too dry. Scale insects can also give trouble but remember that it is not safe to deal with these by applying tar-oil winter wash during the dormant period as the tender, embryo figs would be harmed. In bad cases a summer petroleum wash may be used but it is generally better to attempt hand control using a stiff brush to remove the offending brown scale-like insects.

Any of the fig varieties normally recommended for the open may be

Figs in a heated greenhouse generally produce two crops.

grown under glass—'Brown Turkey', 'Brunswick' and 'White Marseilles', for instance—but with heat available the choice is widened. 'Bourjassotte Grise', 'Negro Largo' and 'Violette Sepor' are all good.

Strawberries

Extra-early strawberries can be obtained quite easily by growing in pots in a heated greenhouse. Fruiting time is governed by when the pots are housed and the night temperature which can be maintained. A minimum temperature of 13°C (55°F) is desirable for ripening and, obviously, much more fuel is necessary to maintain this early in the year than, say, the latter part of April and early May.

The old variety 'Royal Sovereign' is still pre-eminent for this purpose and the first essential is to secure really early-rooted runners. Pot-grown runners should be obtained in July, if possible. Plant them in 15cm (6in) pots using an appropriate pot-

ting compost (mixture) and stand them outdoors on a bed of ashes. The latter prevents worms entering the drainage holes and helps to prevent drying out. The pots should be in full sun and watering will require daily attention. Drying out is fatal.

If the ash bed is deep enough for the pots to be plunged up to their rims, this will protect them from frost and they may stay there until it is time for them to go into the greenhouse. If the pots are exposed, however, it would be better to remove them in November, when growth has ceased, to some sheltered spot such as on the south side of a wall. Lay the pots on their sides and cover with straw to protect them from frost.

Given sufficient heat, plants housed in mid-December may ripen their fruit at the beginning of April and those brought in at the end of January should have ripe berries during the latter half of May.

The strawberry pots should be stood in the lightest position available in the greenhouse. At first no

Early crops of strawberries are possible in a heated greenhouse.

artificial heat should be given and the temperature should be kept down during the daytime, if necessary by free ventilation. No water should be given, but on sunny days the plants should be lightly syringed and the greenhouse atmosphere should be moist rather than dry.

After about two weeks, signs of growth should be observed and a first watering should be given. From now on keep the compost in the pots just nicely moist, judging needs by tapping the pots daily—a ringing sound indicating that the compost is dry, a dull sound that it is wet.

Once the plants are growing freely, the temperature may be permitted to rise very gradually. Aim at a minimum of 7°C (45°F) by night. On sunny days it may still be necessary to give extra ventilation to prevent an undue rise of temperature—liable to encourage the leaves rather than the blossoms.

When the blossom opens, a slightly higher temperature is wanted—up to 10°C (50°F) at night—and syringeing should stop. A buoyant atmosphere will help pollination but nevertheless, as insects are scarce inside a greenhouse at this time of the year, recourse should be made to hand fertilization of the flowers. Around midday, using a camel's hair brush or a small wad of cotton wool, dab the centre of each flower in turn, thus transferring the pollen.

When the fruit has set and the blossom petals have fallen, night temperatures may go up to a minimum of 13°C (55°F), a moister atmosphere may again be permitted and syringeing resumed. This will help, too, to keep the red spider mites at bay. These are often a trouble with forced strawberries and fumigation with smoke is the answer when the infestation is severe.

While the fruits are swelling, a little gentle feeding will be beneficial—weak liquid manure once every 10 days or a commercial liquid fertilizer used according to the manufacturer's instructions.

Once colour shows in the fruit, all feeding must cease, and drier conditions must prevail or botrytis disease will be encouraged: stop syringeing, keep the path drier and give more air. Never, however, allow the pots to dry out. In sunny spring weather watering may be necessary twice a day.

To obtain fruit of top size, thinning is essential. Remove the smallest berries at an early stage and be content with nine berries per pot. Once you have your nine, remove all further blossom. Use little forked pieces of twig or bent galvanized wire

Feed strawberries while they are swelling and thin for top-size fruit.

as props to hold the trusses up and keep the berries in the light and away from the soil or pot side.

Once the berries have been picked the plants are of no further use and should be burned to prevent the spread of red spider mites.

Melons

Belonging to the same genus as the cucumber, the melon requires similar conditions but provides us with one of the most refreshing fruits that can grace our table. Certain varieties of melon may be grown under cloches, in cold frames or in an unheated greenhouse, but in each case a high temperature is necessary for germination and early growth. Where this is unavailable, young plants must be purchased from a specialist grower. The owner of a heated greenhouse, however, can grow a wide range of varieties, secure earlier fruits and, if he chooses, raise plants for fruiting in frames or beneath cloches. This gives him a considerable advantage.

It is possible in warm temperate areas to get ripe melons in April by sowing in November; but as a minimum temperature of 16°C (60°F) is required, this calls for the expenditure of much fuel in the mid-winter months. Few gardeners can contemplate this and most will be content to defer sowing until the end of February or March and have melons in summer rather than spring.

Use 7.5cm (3in) pots and fill with an appropriate potting compost (mixture) or no-soil potting compost, sowing one seed in each and only just covering. A minimum temperature of 21°C (70°F) is necessary for reasonably quick germination—up to 27°C (80°F) if it can be secured—and as bottom heat is best, use, inside the greenhouse, a propagating frame with soil heating if you possess such a thing. Otherwise, try to arrange the seedpots above a hot pipe or heating tube.

Once germination has taken place the temperature may be allowed to fall to 16°C (60°F) during the night.

Four weeks after sowing the roots should be ranging around the edge of the pots, and the young plants ready for transference to their fruiting quarters. These may consist of a box of soil on the staging or, in a glass-to-ground house or one with a very low supporting wall, a bed made up on the border.

Melons require rich soil and good drainage. As they are susceptible to collar rot, it is a good plan to make up the bed in the form of a ridge 45cm (18in) wide at the base and some 38cm (15in) deep. Do not plant deeply; set the plants 60cm (24in) apart.

Strings must be provided to take the melon growth up to the roof wires, as with cucumbers. Stop the shoots, by pinching out the growing points, when 15cm (6in) of growth have been made. This will result in the development of laterals: select two and train them up strings to a height of 2m (6ft) and then stop again.

The embryo melons can be seen as little swellings behind the female flowers. If one is pollinated ahead of the others, it will grow away and later fruit will fail. A good plant should give four good fruits—provided they all start level. To achieve this, remove female blossom until eight open on the same day and then pollinate these by hand about midday, transferring the pollen from the

male flowers to the female with a camel's hair brush or piece of cotton wool.

When the little melons have started swelling, select four of the same size and remove the others. The laterals carrying the chosen fruit should be stopped one joint further on. Also stop the laterals from which any unwanted fruit have been removed.

Aim at keeping the temperature around 18–21°C (65–70°F) during the day, falling no lower than 16°C (60°F) by night. As the spring sunshine warms up, daytime temperatures may rise over 38°C (100°F) but ventilation should always be given as soon as it reaches 27°C (80°F).

Keep the bed uniformly moist and the atmosphere damp by syringeing overhead and damping down the path. The air, however, should be kept somewhat drier when the fruit begins to ripen.

Good varieties for hothouse conditions are 'Best of All' (green flesh), 'Emerald Gem' (green flesh), 'King George' (scarlet flesh) and 'Watermelon Florida Favourite' (pink flesh).

Where the higher temperature cannot be guaranteed, 'Dutch Net'

Left: cantaloupe melons can be grown under cloches or plastic tunnels.
Right: the fruits of climbing melons can be supported with nets.

(orange flesh) and 'Hero of Lockinge' (white flesh) may be relied upon.

Where no artificial heat is available, plants of one or more of the following varieties should be purchased: 'Burpee's Crenshaw' (salmon-pink flesh), 'Charentais' (deep-orange flesh), 'Dutch Net' (orange flesh), 'No Name' (Cantaloupe type with amber-yellow flesh), 'Sweetie' (Cantaloupe type, green flesh, the most likely to prosper in spite of unfavourable weather), and 'Tiger' (orange flesh).

Fruit in pots

Fruit trees may also be grown in the unheated greenhouse in pots, tubs or boxes. The restriction of the roots induces early fruiting and keeps the trees small, while the glass catches the sun's warmth, thus pushing growth forward slightly, protects the blossom and fruitlets from spring frosts and renders protection from birds as the fruit ripens more easily. No artificial heating is necessary; in fact it is inadvisable for apples or pears. Cherries, figs, peaches and plums can be brought along earlier, if desired, by a little additional warmth.

Pot-grown trees raised for this purpose should be bought—apples, sweet cherries, figs, peaches and nectarines, pears, plums and greengages are all available. Start with pots of about 25cm (10in) diameter or boxes of similar dimensions. Crock well to ensure perfect drainage and then cover the crocks with a first layer of compost, rammed down firmly and deep enough for the tree to 'stand' on this with its roots properly spread out and with the top roots just covered. The surface of the soil should be at least 2.5cm (1in) below the pot's rim to allow for watering. Work the compost around the roots, little by little, and firm it down as you proceed with a blunt-ended stick.

For potting compost (mixture) the following formula is recommended by a nursery where they have grown pot trees for over a century: three parts of good fibrous loam, one part of well-rotted manure. To this mixture add one quart-jar of walnut-sized lumps of chalk per barrow-load of compost.

The usual system is to sink the pots in a bed of ashes in the open garden during the winter. Thus treated, the pots will be safe from frost and the ashes will discourage the entry of worms. Outdoors, the wood will ripen better and the cold weather will ensure that the trees have a proper resting period.

At the end of January the pots may be taken into the unheated greenhouse. Ventilate freely during the day in mild weather but shut up early to conserve the sun-heat. Little water will be needed at first—perhaps once in the first week or two and once more in February will be sufficient. In March syringeing will help the buds to break and this should be continued until the fruit begins to colour. Daily syringeing should be resumed after picking, until leaf-fall.

By March more water will be required and this should be given daily attention, testing the pots by tapping. Allow free ventilation when the blossom is open, but avoid draughts. Hand pollination is advisable.

A top-dressing of well-rotted manure should be given when the fruit has all set. Pot trees do not bear very large crops and the fruit will have to be thinned, particularly in the first year or two, to prevent over-cropping. Ventilators should be covered with netting to prevent the entry of

Left: the calamondin, a dwarf orange, makes a decorative pot plant.
Right: figs respond well to pot cultivation and will crop twice in a year.

birds when the fruit begins to ripen.

Each year the pot trees should be repotted in October or November. A little soil is scraped away from the surface and then the pot laid on its side and the tree removed. More soil is then scraped away from the roots and the longest of these are shortened by a third of their length. The tree is then repotted using the same compost formula as before. A larger-size pot should only be provided when absolutely essential; probably the original pots will suffice for two or three seasons and then one size larger, only, should be provided. New trees can be purchased to make use of the first set of pots.

Water once or twice after repotting and about mid-November set the pots outdoors in their winter quarters.

Grapes

The best greenhouse in which a vine is to be grown is one facing south, but there is no reason why other aspects should not be successful, as has often been proved. Span-roofed, three-quarter span and lean-to greenhouses will produce good crops, as well as house porches. The important thing is that the vine plant should get as much sun as possible, especially during the summer and early autumn. Many of the best varieties of vines do best in a heated greenhouse, but there is a wide enough selection to choose

Grapes need as much sun as possible but many varieties do not need heat.

from when no heat is available.

If some heating is installed, it is an advantage to have some means of keeping the atmosphere moist during the growing season by syringeing the plants and soil underneath them frequently—at least once a day. It is not a good practice to spray water on hot pipes as this may result in scorching the young foliage and grapes.

The soil in which the vine plants are to be grown should be as fertile as possible. Where the soil is naturally deep and loamy it may only be necessary to dig in some well-rotted farmyard manure or compost before planting the young vines. Where the soil is not suitable, it is an advantage to remove it, or at least part of it and put in fresh soil. Old turves (sods) which have been weathered for a year or two and allowed to rot down partially, make an excellent foundation for this purpose. Good drainage is also important; vines will not grow well where there is waterlogging at any time. The soil should also contain a certain amount of lime and this can be sprinkled over the surface at the rate of 225g per sq m (8oz per sq yd) while the border is being prepared. If the soil is heavy e.g. clay, drainage can be improved by digging in coarse gravel, or sand as well as organic matter such as peat. Basic slag at 500g per sq m (1lb per sq yd) will also help to improve the texture. Potash is also needed for vines and this can be added in the first case by sprinkling wood ash or burnt garden rubbish over the surface, again while the border is being prepared. Basic slag, as above, supplies phosphates for good root action, but bonemeal can be used instead and this will also supply nitrogen. Bonemeal at 500g per sq m (1lb per sq yd) forked into the surface soil will help. Where the soil is light or gravelly, organic matter will help to retain moisture and many gardeners find it an advantage to mulch the surface of the soil with compost or peat during the growing season. A layer 5cm (2in) deep over the surface will help to cut down loss of water and reduce the need for frequent watering. This mulching should be done each year.

Planting

Most gardeners buy their vine plants from a nursery and these can be planted at almost any time of the year, since they are grown in pots. The best time, however, is in late October or early November. Young plants which have been grown from eyes or cuttings and are well rooted can be planted at the same time. Where the vines are received in pots it is advisable to break the pot, otherwise you may damage the roots when taking them out. When lifting young plants from the open border, lift as much soil as possible around the roots. The reason for early planting in autumn is that the plants are pruned at that time so as to avoid damage from bleeding which takes place when pruning is carried out in late winter and early spring. Should bleeding occur, it can be stopped by binding the cut shoot with painter's knotting.

Soil in the border and around the plant should be moist before planting. Do not set the roots too deeply in the soil; the depth of planting should preferably be that at which they were originally grown in the nursery or pot.

The distance apart depends on the way in which the stems or rods are to be placed. Genrally speaking, vines are best grown with one main stem, when the plants should be set out not less than 1.2m (4ft) apart. This allows the laterals to grow 60cm (2ft) in length. Where vine plants are grown with several stems the distance between these must not be less than 1.2m (4ft).

Dig a hole wide enough to take the roots spread to their fullest extent. If the soil around the roots appears to be unsatisfactory, remove as much as possible. Allow 45cm (18in) from the wall of the greenhouse. A 2m (6ft) cane placed beside each plant will give all the necessary support for the leading shoot and side-shoots for the first year.

Pruning and training

In the spring following planting, young shoots will develop. When these have made six leaves remove the growing point from all except the leading one which will form the rod, and all sub-laterals should be stopped above the first leaf. This treatment should be continued during the summer months, but when the leading shoot has grown 2m (6ft) the growing point should be taken out and all side-shoots pinched above the first leaf, except the top one which will then be allowed to grow on during the summer. Should this existing shoot grow more than 2m (6ft), another cane can be tied to the cross wires which are fixed to the beams across the length of the house, so as to carry an extension of growth of the rod.

To aid pollination of grapes, run the hand gently down embryo bunches.

Stop fruiting laterals 2 leaves beyond the fruit and others after 6 leaves.

Remove all tendrils and pinch out sub-sideshoots in leaf axils.

To encourage well-formed bunches, remove about half the embryo bunches.

A well-grown young vine may reach the roof of the greenhouse by the end of the summer.

When the leaves fall in early November, winter pruning may be done. The leading shoot or rod is cut back to 1-1.2m (3-4ft) from the base according to its vigour. All side-shoots growing from this rod are cut right back to their base. During the winter no heat is necessary, otherwise this may cause bleeding of the vine by encouraging the sap to flow. During the dormant period take the opportunity of cleaning the house thoroughly before new growth begins in March and April. During the winter, also, the opportunity can be taken to put up any special framework on the roof of the greenhouse. A light gauge wire stretched along the length or side of the house and spaced 30cm (12in) apart will give satisfactory support for the vine rod and side-shoots during the following years. Canes can be tied to this wire framework for the first three to four years, depending on the size of the greenhouse, to support the young tender shoots.

In a heated greenhouse, vines can be started into growth in February. Start off with a temperature of 7°C (45°F) raising this by the end of the third week to 16°C (60°F).

This temperature will also suit other plants which may be growing in the house (e.g. azaleas, bulbs) as well as raising seedlings or striking cuttings. Don't allow the temperature to rise above 18°C (65°F) on sunny days, when ventilation should be used. When the buds break, rub out the weakest one, leaving one only on each side-shoot base. After these buds grow out into new lateral shoots and a bunch of fruit has set, the lateral should be stopped by pinching the shoot at the second leaf past the bunch. During this time the leading shoot will be growing and making new side-shoots which should be shortened as already described in the work for the first year. Side-shoots from the rod can be tied to the wire framework with raffia. Should bleeding of the wounds result from pruning, cover the cut surfaces either with a vine styptic or seal with a red-hot iron or cover with a layer of sealing wax. Provided the soil is in reasonably good condition all that should be required is a top-dressing of well-rotted manure when the vines are starting into growth, or a dressing of bone-meal at 125-250g per sq m (4-8oz per sq yd) given over the border. In addition, one of the special vine fertilizers may be used, applied according to the manufacturer's instructions in April. During the summer months ventilate the greenhouse adequately and at the first sign of mildew on the leaves, spray with thiram to control.

Vines in unheated greenhouses should not be started into growth until March or early April and the same care should be taken with regard to feeding, ventilation and spraying.

Sufficient water must also be given to moisten the soil thoroughly, though where the roots are allowed to grow outside the house there may be less need for this than where the roots are growing inside. Mulching with organic matter will help to reduce the need for watering.

At the end of the growing season— August, early September—less ventilation should be given, so that warmth will help to ripen the grapes. Remove surplus shoots, so that light gets to the berries.

When the main rod has reached the top of the house it should be pruned each year, the leading shoot removed completely and all laterals on the main rod pruned back to one or two eyes during the dormant periods. Space out the laterals or spurs so that these are not less than 30cm (12in) apart. After a few years the spurs become large and should be reduced in length as much as possible. Occasionally, these old spurs will put out a young growth from near their base and they can be cut back to this point.

Thinning
Berries or bunches are ready for thinning from twelve to fifteen days after the fruitlets have begun to form and it is much better to start the thinning early than to leave the job until the fruits are nearly full size. Use a forked stick and a fine pair of scissors. Special vine scissors are obtainable from horticultural suppliers.

Grapes should be cut when they are fully mature and handled with care. To maintain ripe grapes in a good condition for a long time requires skill and care. They can be left on the plants and the house kept as cool as possible, with a little heat to dispel damp. Some gardeners cut the bunches from the rod with a portion of the stem and insert the end of the stem in a bottle filled with water. In this way they will keep for some weeks.

Vines in a mixed house
It is possible to grow good crops of vines with other plants. Plants or creepers must not be allowed to grow but, of course, those plants which must have a good deal of light will suffer during the summer.

Shady conditions, however, suit such plants as ferns, begonias, fuchsias, gloxinias and are not too unfavourable for perpetual carnations, pelargoniums, and some cacti.

Tomatoes are not a good crop to grow under vines, since they require more light and a drier atmosphere.

Vines in pots
Some gardeners grow vines in pots, and apart from being plunged outdoors during the autumn and winter, their general treatment is the same as that recommended for vines growing indoors, though of course, the rod is kept very much shorter and grown in an upright fashion. The rod may be no more than 1-1.2m (3-4ft) long.

Propagation
Vines can be propagated by eyes or cuttings (see page 119). Cuttings should be 30cm (12in) long and inserted to half their length in good soil in November or December. Vine eyes can be propagated in a greenhouse or warm place.

Vines are self-fertile and there is no problem with pollination.

Conclusion
As well as bearing choice fruit, grape vines are well worth growing for their highly ornamental foliage; indeed, even the leaves can be used in cooking.

Frames and cloches (Hotkaps)

A garden frame allows you to grow plants in carefully controlled conditions of light, temperature, humidity and ventilation. Basically, a frame consists of a low rectangular box with a transparent lid, but there are a number of different designs and they can be made in a variety of materials.

There are many advantages to having a frame in your garden. If you have no greenhouse, a frame is a great asset, for you can grow almost as many different kinds of fruit and vegetables in a good, properly managed frame as you can in a greenhouse. Vegetable seedlings can be raised successfully. You will be able to grow superb cucumbers, melons, peppers and other delicate produce, as well as such out of season vegetables as early cauliflowers or early tomatoes from low-growing, bushy plants. A frame also provides a suitable place for drying off and resting plants, for ripening crops like onions, and for giving winter protection to tender and half-hardy plants.

If you do have a greenhouse, a frame is a must for hardening off: seedlings raised in a greenhouse can be transferred in their containers to a frame and gradually exposed to the more rigorous outdoor atmosphere. Most important, a frame can be used to relieve the pressure on greenhouse space, which can then be devoted to more urgent needs.

Types of frame
There are many different types of frame. Most frames have a deep back and a shallow front and some sort of covering light. Although dimensions vary considerably, there should always be adequate room between the tops of the plants and the covering light. The two most common types of frame in general use are the lean-to and the span-roof.

Lean-to frames A lean-to frame has a high back wall and a low front wall connected by sloping side walls. The frame is closed with a glazed light (window), which you either slide open or prop open to control ventilation.

There are two types of lights: English and Dutch. The English type is rather like a window frame, usually made from fairly heavy wood with a number of small panes of glass held in place by wooden glazing bars or window frames. It usually slides open on runners.

A Dutch light is just as effective, but it is cheaper to buy and easier to handle. It usually consists of one sheet of glass held in grooves in a wooden framework. The lights are usually opened by lifting them from the front and can be kept open by means of wooden blocks or props. There is no putty, which makes replacing broken glass an easy task.

On the other hand, the panes are large and more expensive to replace than the small panes of the English lights.

Span-roof frames A span-roof frame looks like a small greenhouse, and it is particularly useful for growing taller plants such as peas or some varieties of tomato. The low walls are joined together on either side by gabled ends connected by a ridge, so that the frame is higher in the middle than on the sides. The lights are attached to the frame by wires or hinges, and they usually open upwards.

This type has two advantages over the lean-to: it allows a more even distribution of light and it is easier to control the ventilation within. It can also be used for a wider range of purposes. However, it is more ex-

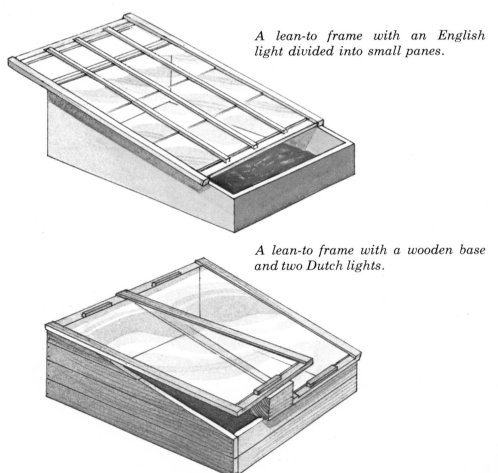

A lean-to frame with an English light divided into small panes.

A lean-to frame with a wooden base and two Dutch lights.

pensive and less portable than a lean-to frame, so regard it as a long-term investment.

The choice of materials

Frames can be made of wood, metal, bricks or concrete; and the lights can be either glass or plastic.

Redwood or cedar are the best choices for wooden frames, particularly cedar as it is resistant to rot and does not need to be painted. A soft wood frame must be painted or treated with preservative if it is to stand up to outdoor conditions. Never use creosote for preserving the wood, as it can be toxic to plants. There are several horticultural wood preservatives available.

Metal frames, particularly aluminium ones, have several advantages over wooden ones. They are very light and easy to move, and they require almost no maintenance. However, they are usually glazed to the ground to admit the maximum amount of light, and this makes them difficult to keep warm in winter.

Brick and concrete frames are the easiest to keep warm, but they are, of course, permanent structures which cannot be moved. Modern designs of collapsible plastic and fibreglass frames are extremely light to move and they are quite useful in the small garden because they are easy to store. However, they tend not to be very satisfactory in the coldest weather.

Glass is the best material for the lights, although it is becoming popular to use heavy-weight plastic instead. Plastic is cheaper and lighter, and it is not brittle and as likely to break as glass, an important consideration if small children play in your garden. However, plastic transmits slightly less light than glass, it loses heat more rapidly than glass and condensation remains on the inside surface, cutting down the amount of light that can get through to the plants. Efficient ventilation is extremely important with plastic and it needs to be replaced quite frequently, sometimes every year.

Heated frames

Frames are usually unheated, but the development of safe electric warming cables has made it quite easy to convert cold frames into heated ones by laying cables in the soil or around the walls. Adding heat increases the versatility of the frame considerably, making it in effect a miniature greenhouse. Coupled to a reliable rod thermostat, the system becomes fully automatic and very reasonable in its running costs.

Another sort of heated frame can be made by placing a frame on a hot-bed in which fresh manure has been allowed to rot. The manure should be covered with a layer of soil so that the heat does not become too intense for the plants; it will also prevent rotting of the bases of wooden seedboxes. However, electrical heating is easier and cleaner.

In cold weather, and particularly at night, heated frames can be given extra protection by placing sheets of canvas, hessian (burlap) or matting over the glass. Straw or several thicknesses of heavy-grade plastic sheeting can be used also. Whichever covering you use, remove it as soon as possible to allow light and air into the frame.

Positioning the frame

It is very important to put the frame in the best possible growing position. Ideally it should face south. If this is not possible, choose a site where it is protected from any cold prevailing winds and where it will receive the maximum amount of sunlight. Always put your frame on well-drained ground, never on a spot where water tends to accumulate.

If you plan to use a frame in conjunction with your greenhouse for hardening off, then place them close together so that the plants need not be carried far. If the frame is to be heated, position it close to the electricity supply to minimize installation costs.

Preparing the soil

The soil for the frame needs careful preparation. The area should be cut out to a depth of 30–40cm (12–16in), and the bottom of the hole covered with a 10cm (rin) layer of fine rubble

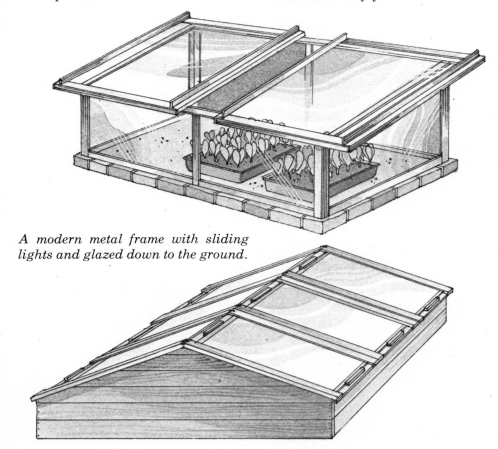

A modern metal frame with sliding lights and glazed down to the ground.

A span-roof frame is useful for propagation, for instance, of shrubs.

Above: cuttings of shrubs and her-baceous plants set in rows in a frame.

Below: an electrical propagating frame can fit into the greenhouse.

and weathered cinders. If the subsoil is heavy, break it up with a fork before putting in the drainage material. The rest of the hole should be filled with a specially prepared compost, either home-made or commercial. The formula you use will depend on whether you intend to raise seedlings in the frame or grow plants to maturity in it. In small frames it is a good idea to use seed trays or pots for seed raising and to grow plants to maturity in the prepared frame soil.

Frame gardening

To grow successfully, the plants in a frame must be given special care. Watering, ventilation, shading and protection from the cold are all important.

Rain is not usually allowed to fall on plants in a frame, so artificial watering is necessary. One method is mist irrigation, which involves a rigid plastic water pipe fixed to the frame roof. The pipe, which can be connected to an ordinary hosepipe, has a series of brass nozzles which provide an even, fine mist of water. Another method, particularly good if you are growing melons or cucumbers, is to use 13cm (5in) clay pots. Sink these into the ground to half their depth, about 53cm (21in) away from the plants, and keep them filled with water.

Ventilation of a frame is very important for healthy plants. Controlled ventilation will reduce temperature and control humidity, eliminating condensation. The frame light should be opened on the leeward side when cold winds prevail. With a Dutch light this is generally done by raising the light to the required height and propping it open with a stepped block or brick. Ventilate an English light by sliding the glass backwards or forwards the required distance.

Shading is another method of controlling temperature within the frame. This can be done simply by covering the glass with muslin, cheesecloth, an old net curtain or any similar light-textured material. A more permanent method is to make a wooden window frame of a size that can be fixed over the light. Fix laths across the frame, spaced about 4cm (1½in) apart. When needed, this lathed frame can be placed over the light.

In severe wintry weather it will be necessary to protect the plants in a frame from frost and to conserve heat as much as you can. During a very cold spell, cover the frame with blankets, rugs, coconut matting or a thick layer of straw.

Sometimes strong winds can damage plants in an open frame, birds or insect pests may get in and cause damage, or dead leaves may be blown in and smother young plants. These dangers can be minimized with a fine plastic or wire mesh screen placed over the opening when the light is raised.

It is important to keep your frame clean and well maintained. Clean the glass frequently both inside and out, to admit the maximum amount of light and to discourage pests and diseases. Keep your frame free of any garden debris such as pots or boxes, decaying plants or weeds, which might harbour pests and diseases.

The fabric of the frame must always be kept in good condition. Treat the wood with preservative and white-wash bricks or concrete annually. Replace any broken or cracked glass immediately. If you have a heated frame, regularly check all electrical equipment or wiring for faults. A frame which is not in top condition will not give good results so proper maintenance is essential.

Growing in a heated frame

In a heated frame maintained at a temperature of 15-21°C (60–70°C), it almost any fruit or vegetables throughout the winter. Tomatoes, dwarf French beans, strawberries and forced rhubarb can all be enjoyed if you manage your frame carefully.

A heated frame can be used instead of a greenhouse for raising seedlings of such vegetables as marrows (squash), cucumbers, celery and celeriac, which do better if given some heat. It is also possible to grow mushrooms. Total darkness is not necessary, but you must keep the frame shaded from direct sunlight.

What kind of frame?

A number of key factors should in-

Radishes are quick growing and make a good crop for the cold frame.

fluence your choice of a garden frame. The sort of cultivation you intend to carry out is one consideration. For example, if you want a frame for hardening off seedlings and cuttings or producing early supplies of low-growing crops, then a relatively simple, low, lean-to type is quite adequate. On the other hand, if you want to raise tall plants like tomatoes in the frame, you will find a tall, span-roof type is much more satisfactory. You have to balance this advantage in terms of cultivation against greater expense and the fact that this type of frame is sometimes difficult to position in a small garden, because the ridge of the roof should run north to south to get the best results.

If you want to use a frame only for a short period of the year, say in late winter and spring to grow out-of-season vegetables, the best choice is a lightweight metal-framed, type, possibly with plastic glazing, so that it can be easily moved and stored away when not in use.

If you are thinking in terms of a heated frame, avoid an all-glass structure or one with metal base walls, since they lose heat easily. Base walls of wood, brick, concrete or thick asbestos sheeting are better.

Using your cold frame

Perhaps the most valuable use to which you can put your cold frame is for hardening off seedlings that have started in a greenhouse. In this process delicate young plants are gradually encouraged to tolerate the rigours of outdoor conditions. This must be a slow and careful process to avoid causing shock to the plants. A frame is ideal for the job because the temperature, light, heat and humidity can be readily controlled. A wide variety of plants are hardened off in this way, including such vegetables as early peas, celeriac and asparagus peas, which are usually germinated under glass.

A cold frame is ideal for raising seedlings for early crops outdoors or for producing out-of-season vegetables, which must remain in the frame from sowing to harvest time. To produce out-of-season crops, choose only varieties recommended by the seedsman for that purpose. Because conditions in a frame favour good germination and growing, sow lightly, with consequently less thinning. Vegetables which can be grown in a frame for early harvesting include asparagus, beet, dwarf French beans, carrots, cauliflowers, lettuce, marrows (squash), spring onions (scallions), peas, sweet corn (corn) and turnips. To obtain early crops in some cases it is necessary to sow in autumn, and a frame then affords good winter protection to the young plants.

Several of the more luxurious vegetables and fruits which usually have to be grown in a greenhouse can be satisfactorily produced in a cold frame in summer. These include melons, cucumbers, peppers and aubergines (eggplants). If you plan to grow any of these, consider the amount of headroom they require when choosing a frame. It might be worthwhile reserving a separate tall frame just for these crops.

The question of size of course depends on the space available in your garden. Sometimes it is better to install two smallish frames in convenient corners than to try and accommodate one large frame. In any case, it is not wise to have a light more than 1.4m (4½ft) from back to front, as anything bigger becomes rather unwieldy and a great accident risk. Rather than exceed this size, it is better to have several smaller frames placed next to each other.

If you settle for a lean-to portable frame, it is still possible to create additional height. You can stand the base on several courses of bricks or on a wall of consolidated soil, or place the frame over a pit, about 30cm (1ft) deep, with the other dimensions 15-23cm (6-9in) less than those of the frame base.

Making your own frame

With the wide choice of frames now commercially available, you will probably find it quite easy to buy the particular size and type of frame for your individual needs. If you cannot afford to make this investment,

however, it is a relatively simple job to construct your own frame, and this will ensure that it is of the right size to suit your garden.

A frame without a base

As a last resort, providing you can obtain a suitable glazed light, and providing that your soil is not water-logged, you can frame-garden successfully without even a base. All you have to do is to dig a rectangular pit of the appropriate size in a sunny spot in the garden and fill it to within 30cm (1ft) of the top with a rich soil and then cover it at ground level with your light. To support the light, it is advisable to edge the pit with bricks or paving stones.

Making a heated frame

There is no doubt that a heated frame has very much greater scope than one that is permanently cool. There are several ways of making one: we describe the traditional 'hot-bed' method and the more modern electrical method.

Making a hot-bed This is an old-fashioned but effective method of heating a frame. One essential ingredient of such a bed is fresh manure. Unfortunately this is a commodity that many people find difficult to obtain nowadays. Anybody who can get it, however, has a very cheap and effective method of heating a frame.

To make a hot-bed, fresh strawy manure, not more than 21 days old, is mixed with about one-third of its weight of fairly recently fallen, dry leaves. The leaves keep the mass from becoming too hot and 'burning' the roots of plants put in it. About half of a load of manure is the amount needed for an average-sized frame.

It is normal to stack the heap for up to 14 days, during which time it is turned over four or five times. A little water should be added to it to prevent it becoming too dry. After this period the fermentation caused by the bacteria in the heap will produce enough heat.

In the meantime an area, with dimensions about 45cm (18in) greater than those of the frame, is chosen as a site. For a guide in spreading the manure, each corner of this space

should be marked by a stake driven into the ground. Over this area, spread a 15cm (6in) layer of manure mixture, first shaken up then beaten down with a fork and firmed by treading to create a uniformly well-compacted bed. Two or three more 15cm (6in) layers should be added successively and treated the same.

After the bed has been made, the frame base should be sited centrally on the heap. Leave it open for a few days to allow steam and fumes to escape. Next, add a level, well-firmed 15-23cm (6-9in) layer of good soil. After about a day this will have warmed to the temperature of the hot-bed. When it has fallen to 24°C (75°F) you can start sowing. The bed will stay warm for at least two months.

Heating by electricity A very efficient method of heating a frame is the use of soil-warming cables, which can be purchased in various lengths and easily installed. The shortest is 6m (20ft) with a loading of 75 watts, which is adequate for heating soil in a frame 0.5-1 sq m (6-12 sq ft) in area; the next size is double in length and has a loading of 150 watts, which makes it suitable for an area of 1.4-2.2 sq m (15-24 sq ft). These should meet the needs of most amateurs.

A hot-bed is easily made in a frame by laying the soil-warming cable 20-25cm (8-10in) below the level of the soil surface in lengthwise loops with about 15cm (6in) between the runs, avoiding any sharp bends or cross wires, and connecting it securely to the main power supply. On top of it is placed the layer of soil. It is important always to keep the soil damp to ensure an even distribution of warmth.

For a propagating bed, the soil in the frame should be excavated for a depth of 8.75cm (3½in). On the area to be used for this purpose, lay a 3.75cm (1½in) layer of well-firmed sand (*on no account* use insulating materials, such as peat, vermiculite, fibre, ash, clinker and moss because they are liable to cause the cable to overheat). The soil-warming cable is laid out as above on the surface of this sand and covered with a further 5cm (2in) of sand. Seed boxes are stood on the sand and packed tight together; pots are plunged about 6mm ($\frac{1}{4}$in) into the sand and 2cm ($\frac{3}{4}$in) of damp granulated peat is packed between them.

It is usual for the soil warmth to be controlled by the 'dosage' method: by switching on the cables for about 10 hours nightly. Experience will soon indicate whether any modification is necessary.

If you want to heat the air in the frame, this can be done by purchasing a kit containing an air-warming cable (which is rather similar to a soil-warming one), stainless steel mounting clips and screws. For air-warming, twice as much heat is needed as for soil-warming, which means that the length of the cable required has to be doubled. The other essential for air-warming is thermostatic control. The air-warming cable is run around the inside walls of the frame, with a 2.5cm (1in) spacing between each strand. It is attached to the wall by means of mounting clips.

Cloches

The true cloche, bell-jar or Hotkap, which was developed in France as an important aid in the early production of market garden crops, is seldom seen in the modern garden. Its place is now largely taken by the badly named continuous cloche in which sheets of glass are wired together to form a miniature glass case. The true cloche had some advantages to offset its great cost; it was quite air-tight and its considerable stability and weight made it proof against all that the stormiest weather could bring. Where cuttings have to be given summer rooting treatment the bell-glass or cloche is superior to the so-called continuous cloche as a close, humid atmosphere is secured with ease. However, the design and use of the modern cloche has resulted in greater versatility and a new conception of protected cultivation.

There are a large number of designs or types available today and all use either glass or a plastic material in their construction. The basic design of a cloche is a simple

Two types of cloche and between them a flexible plastic tunnel.

frame work of wire or metal which supports sheets of glass or plastic. Some designs are extremely simple; others complicated with opening panels. All metal parts are suitably weatherproofed.

Glass types

The simplest design is a tent shape and consists of two sheets of glass supported by a single wire bent to a tent shape. The bottom ends of the wire are bent to hold the glass and a specially designed wire handle clips the glass into place at the top.

The barn cloche is next in design with four sheets of glass if a pitched roof is required, or three sheets if a flat-roof design is preferred. In the former model the wire framework is, of necessity, a little more complicated, especially in some types which have ventilator panels or removable sheets. The main supporting wire conforms to the shape of a barn with the bottom ends bent slightly to hold the bottom edge of the side sheets of glass. Two eave wires are placed under the main wire and clip over the top edges of the roof glass to hold them in position against the main

wire. The bottom edges of the roof sheets rest in the eave wires and are held in place at the top or apex of the glass roof by a special wire handle which, in some designs, has a special extension piece to allow one roof panel to open against it in several positions.

There is usually a standard length for the cloche glass of 60cm (2ft); the width varies according to the size of the cloche required. Generally there are two main sizes, 15cm (6in) and 30cm (12in). All glass is 70g (2$\frac{1}{2}$oz), the standard quality for general horticultural purposes.

Several designs employ a flat roof and are usually wider than those just described. All use three sheets of glass in their assembly, a roof sheet and two side ones. Support for the glass is either strong galvanized wire or angled strip metal. The method of supporting the glass is generally very similar to that used in the barn cloches. The glass is slightly larger than tent or barn glass and more headroom is available. The tallest type of flat-roof cloche uses 60cm (2ft) square glass for the sides and a 30cm (12in) wide sheet for the roof. Glass cloches vary in assembled width from about 23cm (9in) to 60cm (2ft).

Plastic types

There are two types of plastic cloche, those made from thin polythene material and others manufactured in more rigid plastic or PVC materials. Both have the great advantage of lightness and strength.

Cloches made from the thinner materials are framed by thin gauge galvanized wire which is preformed into a tent or semicircular shape. This wire framework usually extends a few inches at the base of the cloche to provide anchorage feet which are inserted into the ground. Some of the thicker gauge plastics are shaped by being sandwiched in metal sections or framing.

The lengths of plastic cloches vary considerably from about 45cm (18in) to as much as 90cm (3ft). Widths vary also but generally a measurement of about 45cm (18in) seems to be popular.

Home-made cloches

Cloches can easily and cheaply be made at home if some strong wire and a sheet of polythene are purchased. There are usually three grades of polythene available – standard, medium and heavy. All are suitable, although the heavy type should weather better. Various cloche widths can be made up as the polythene is sold in widths from 60cm (2ft) to 3.6m (12ft). The wire is used to form hoops of the required height and width. These are pushed into the ground along the row to be covered. A spacing of about 60cm (2ft) between each hoop is usually sufficient. The plastic sheet is then laid over the hoops and the edges and ends trapped under the soil by about 7.5cm (3in).

For extra protection the plastic can be doubled before it is placed over the hoops. It is essential, of course, to purchase only the clearest grade of plastic for cloche construction.

There are special wire- or metal-reinforced plastic or PVC materials available and these can be cut easily to any desired size. They can then be bent to form cloches of various shapes. It will be necessary to make wire pegs so that these can be pushed through the bottom edges of the cloches and into the soil to secure them.

The selection of cloches

The selection of a cloche will depend on the type of work it has to do and the cost. Plastic cloches are cheap to buy, light to handle but do not provide good frost protection. Their average life span is not as long as that of glass cloches unless the more expensive, thicker gauge plastic is used. When not required, plastic cloches can be stacked in a very small area.

The glass cloches give more pro-

tection and more use can be made of them in the winter. They are more substantial and are easier to use.

Some cloche manufacturers provide special adaptors so that certain models can be given extra height. The adaptors usually consist of special strong wires and extra sheets of glass, the same length as that of the cloche and about 30cm (1ft) wide. Four wires and two sheets of glass are required for each cloche. Two wires are inserted at each side of the cloche and a few inches in from each end. A sheet of glass is inserted under the wires on each side to form two walls and the cloche is placed on top of the four wires in special grooves. The cloches are, in fact, on stilts with the gaps at the sides filled in with the two extra sheets of glass.

Glass is easily broken but is otherwise long-lasting; however plastic is used increasingly for cloches, as above, and tunnels, as below.

Garden rooms

While many gardens do not have space for greenhouses, many home owners are able to utilize house space to make what are in effect garden rooms. They may be little more than glass corridors or small porches, but with care than can provide the right conditions and the space for growing a fairly wide range of plants that could also be grown in greenhouse conditions.

Sun rooms

If you should want to extend your house by building a sun room or sun porch or by enclosing a patio, it should be designed to collect as much sunlight as possible, and be situated on the side of the house which faces the sun for most of the day. In the northern hemisphere this will be the south side, and in the southern hemisphere the north.

Basing the position of the main window as near to south or north as possible will provide the maximum total number of hours of sunlight inside the room, but you may prefer to vary this a little to suit your own needs. If the room is likely to be empty during the morning and only used in the afternoon and early evening, it night be better to face the main windows to the south-west, or even due west in countries where the days are very long in summer (this includes Britain). But if you intend to use the room intermittently all day, a main south window will probably offer the best solution. Depending on the position of the sun room in the house, it may be possible to have a smaller window in the west wall as well, or even in both east and west walls.

Although the orientation of the room (which determines the quantity of sunlight) is often the major factor in siting a sun room, the view is also important, and may to a certain extent override orientation in deciding the location of the room and its windows. If the southern outlook is poor, but that to the east or west more attractive, it may be worth sacrificing some sunlight in order to enjoy a pleasant view. Though a north window alone could not catch any sun in the northern countries, an additional window in a north wall looking out to a sunlit garden beyond the immediate shadow of the house, may be worth considering as a

Foliage and flowering plants soften the appearance of a sunroom.

second window position in conjunction with a main west or (where possible) south window.

Remember that tall trees, especially if fairly near the house, could obstruct sunlight. The sun's angle is much lower in winter than in summer, and a tree which may be well below the sun in midsummer and throw only a short shadow could cut out the sun during the winter months when the shadow will stretch much further. This is especially true of evergreen trees.

Another factor to be borne in mind is also an external one: the question of exposure. In northern hemisphere countries, for example, such as Britain and the United States, north-facing sites are likely to be much more exposed to cold winds than south-facing ones, although other factors such as nearby walls and buildings can affect this. The cold winds will reduce the inside temperature of the room mostly during the winter months, when it will only be used internally, but may also be a disadvantage in summer when the room will normally be used in conjuction with outside seating on a terrace.

So a clump of tall evergreen trees which could represent a shadow nuisance on the south side of a garden may be a decided advantage as a windbreak along the north or east side, where their shadows will fall away from the house in the afternoon anyway. If there are no such trees it may be worth planting some, and using a temporary additional screen until they grow tall enough to be effective. This can also be made up of natural planting, for instance quick-growing plants that can be removed later.

Alternatively, it can consist of a perforated wall made from precast concrete screen wall units, or an open timber screen with climbing plants. If two alternative positions seem equally suitable as far as these points are concerned, other factors can be decisive. Something which could tip the balance in favour of one site or the other is the existing wall pattern. If one position involves building against a flat wall and the other in an internal angle between two existing walls, the second has the advantage of requiring the building of only two new walls instead of three. Apart from the resultant saving in construction cost, a room in an internal angle is more comfortable and less expensive to heat, as it has only two external walls instead of three. It also offers two directions of access from the main house instead of one.

This factor of access is another major consideration. When a new room is being built into an external wall, it is often hard to give it an independent entrance from the hall that does not involve going through another room. So it may be necessary to approach the sun room through an existing room. Many people find access through a living or dining room acceptable, but if you do not, and practical considerations prevent entry through other rooms such as study or kitchen, the only solution is to cut a new corridor by partitioning off 90cm (3ft) wide strip of an existing room between the hall and sun room.

You will also have to think about the effect the sun room will have on the room or rooms adjacent to it. In a house with large rooms, there may be a piece of solid external wall long enough to accommodate the whole of the new room without cutting into existing windows. In most cases, however, and particularly since the sun room will normally have its longer side parallel with the external wall, at least part of an existing window or external door is affected.

If this is the only source of light to the existing room, the addition of the new room will seriously reduce the level of daylight even if the window is only partly blocked. You can compensate for this by creating a new window in a wall not affected by the new room. Sometimes, if the existing rooms have high ceilings, a clerestory window can be cut in the external wall of the inside room over the roof of the sun room, allowing direct high-level lighting.

If neither of these solutions is practicable, you can ensure that ample light enters indirectly from the sun room by using large windows in

the wall adjoining the inside room. You will have to open up most of the area of the wall between the old and new rooms in order to admit as much light as possible, The use of rooflights in the sun room roof, as mentioned later, can also help to boost light to an inside room lit in this way.

In summer, the sun room will probably be used for many activities, and you will tend to use it in conjunction with the garden, so there will be fairly heavy traffic in and out. In the cold months, on the other hand, you are more likely to use it for sitting in to enjoy a touch of sunlight. So you should choose finishes, especially for the floor, which are tough enough to withstand traffic from the garden yet comfortable enough to make an attractive retreat in spring and autumn.

You will probably want to use your sun room in conjunction with the garden in summer, and a paved

A well-planned garden room can link the house and the garden proper.

terrace surrounding it can be very useful, both as a dry and level area for sitting and for children to play on, and for reducing the dirt carried into the house from the garden itself. The terrace should be wide enough to enjoy plenty of sun, allowance being made for the shadow of the other parts of the house, and screened from cold winds. It should be on one continuous level as far as possible, with only a fall of about 1 in 60 to throw off rainwater. Small terraces can be drained by sloping them away from the house towards the garden, but large terraces should fall to a central gully with a drain leading to a main drain.

Conservatories
Strictly speaking, conservatories are display houses for plants which have been raised and grown elsewhere, though there is not the

slightest reason why the sun room or conservatory should not be pressed into service for simple propagation and other jobs for which an ordinary greenhouse might be used. The only trouble is that used in this way, clutter can spoil the effect.

Conservatories of reasonable size are not expensive to build. They are easy to look after, and give remarkable scope for the gardener to grow a variety of hardy and not so hardy plants.

Near-greenhouse conditions, ideal for growing and rejuvenation, can easily be arranged by installing simple heating systems. Sometimes, in the warmer parts of the country or where the conservatory has a warm aspect in a sheltered position, the heat from the house is sufficient.

A solid floor makes it possible to keep a thriving, humid atmosphere by the simple means of damping down. Heat without humidity can be fatal to plants; moist, warm conditions help to keep most of them at the peak of condition.

Where there is staging to stand the pots on, it should be strong enough to carry a layer of shingle.

Suitable plants

Greenhouse plants which enjoy

With careful planning a garden can be colourful all year.

temperate conditions thrive in conservatories. These include cinerarias, coleus, various primulas such as *P. obconica* and *P. malocoides*, the very showy greenhouse calceolarias such as the 'Albert Kent Hybrids', *C. multiflora nana* and 'Victoria Prize'.

Cyclamen, many begonias, certainly many of the highly ornamental, scented-leaved pelargoniums can be grown as well as a wide range of cacti and other succulents. In fact by careful selection and sensible control of heating and other conditions, there need seldom be a time when there is nothing of colour or interest to see. Annuals in pots should not be overlooked; delightful annuals such as schizanthus, mignonette, salpiglossis, clarkia and calendula.

Hanging baskets, which might otherwise be buffeted about, can find true expression in an enclosed area where there is room to avoid collision. Ordinary hanging basket plants, lobelia, tagetes, nasturtiums, geraniums and fuchsias and so on, will thrive to perfection, provided extra attention is paid to watering. Fuchsias and pelargoniums, of course, can be used as individual displays throughout the staging.

Hoya bella and *Hoya carnosa* are two plants which will permanently occupy a hanging basket with great success. And if a little extra care is taken, a warm corner might well see *Columnia gloriosa* doing quite well, though strictly speaking this does prefer rather warmer conditions than a conservatory can usually provide. The two hoyas, despite their somewhat exotic appearance, are really quite hard-wearing and will even endure ordinary living-room conditions if they have to: although not every living room is always quite right.

A place will have to be found for various ferns. A shady spot, perhaps, beneath the staging.

There is considerable scope for climbing plants. Where there is sufficient room, the passion flower – *Passiflora caerulea* – can hardly be left out. *Cobaea scandens* has great attraction, and with just that extra warmth and protection that the conservatory can provide, here is a fine chance to grow the deliciously fragrant *Jasminum polyanthum* with its large trusses of dainty white blossom.

So many of the plants suitable for these under-cover conditions (both annual and perennial) grow well enough outside in the garden, as will have been recognized, but afforded just that extra welcome offered by the conservatory or sunroom they can realize a potential that, subjected to the weather, especially in

Pelargoniums, often called geraniums, are excellent garden-room plants. *Both 'Doris Frith' (above) and 'Degata' (below) are long-flowering.*

a bad season, they could possibly never know. And many pot plants traditionally suited to the rough justice handed out by the ordinary living room, will nevertheless make an even better showing in more controlled conditions.

A wide range of bulbs come into the reckoning, not least some of the hardy kinds to be brought on early. Give warmth and light after the statutory period of cool and dark elsewhere, and it is very useful all around if a conservatory can be run in conjunction with cold frames.

Fuchsias are among the most useful and colourful greenhouse plants.

Propagation

Propagation is simply the increasing of plants from the parent stock. By increasing your own plants rather than buying new stock you will not only derive great satisfaction but also save money in the process. This is especially true of the propagation of vegetables, shrubs, annuals, perennials and bedding plants.

The usual method is by production and sowing of seed, but in many cases plants do not come true from seed, especially hybrid plants. Therefore to perpetuate particularly attractive plants it may be necessary to propagate vegetatively, that is by division, suckers, cuttings, layering and budding.

Equipment

A greenhouse is not essential to the process of propagation, but because you can create particularly suitable conditions within one, the process is generally more successful. Similarly, those fortunate enough to have a frame in addition, will be able to harden off their seedlings outside and increase the amount of space within the greenhouse. Other useful pieces of equipment are a propagating unit, a mist propagator, and of course, pots and seed and potting composts (mixtures).

Seeds and sowing

Seeds today should give you quality, variety and save you money. The story of plant breeding is one of constant improvement. New varieties are continually being developed to give better flavour, colour, size, hardiness, resistance to disease and higher yields. As well as these advantages, when you raise your own plants from seed you have full control over their initial growth and development, crucial stages which affect the quality of the resulting plants.

A wide range of vegetables and decorative plants can be raised from seeds.

The period between sowing seed and the first appearance of the seedlings is known as *germination*.

Choosing and buying seeds

Seeds are living things. If they are too old, or have been stored in a place where the atmosphere is damp so that they rot, or have been exposed to too much heat, they may lose the ability to germinate so buy only from reputable seedsmen.

Some seeds are packed in special humidity-controlled, airtight, watertight, heat- and cold-resistant sealed packets, so that they reach you in a perfectly fresh condition. The seeds in these packets will remain fresh for a very long time but, once the packets are opened and the seeds exposed to the air, they will deteriorate. Sowing should then be done as soon as possible.

When ordering your seeds, send your list off to the seedsmen early in the year, as choice varieties often sell out quickly. If you buy your seeds from a garden centre or shop, look carefully at the date stamp on the packet and do not buy old seed.

Pelleted seed

A very useful recent advantage is pelleted seed, though this is available only for the more popular varieties of common vegetables. Each seed is coated with an inert, clay-like material (sometimes with fungicides or pesticides added to counteract soil-borne pests and diseases) that increases their size enormously. Each seed is at the centre of what appears to be a small greyish pill, so that it is easy to pick up and sow individually. This is particularly useful with very small seeds or very light seeds.

Because pelleted seeds are so easy to handle, they can be spaced at precise distances apart, so that you do not need to carry out the tedious operation of thinning and so on.

The clay-like coat softens and expands on contact with moisture. Some gardeners have experienced a high failure rate with pelleted seeds; this is usually the result of applying either too little or too much water.

F₁ hybrids

F_1 hybrid seed is well worth the

A small electrically heated propagator is inexpensive to run and greatly extends the usefulness of a greenhouse.

extra cost. F_1 hybrids are produced by crossing two specially selected parent plants chosen for their desirable characteristics, and this is usually done by hand pollination or other special techniques, which is why you have to pay more for them. However, F_1 hybrids give higher yields, are more disease-resistant, more uniform in appearance and usually earlier maturing. You should never attempt to save seed yourself from F_1 hybrids as it will not produce plants true to type.

Hardiness and time of sowing

The time of year at which the seeds of a particular plant should be sown depends on the plants hardiness, which in turn depends on whether it originally comes from a cool or a warm climate and often on the particular variety. If you are unfamiliar with the variety, you should check sowing time with the seed catalogue.

The earliness of sowing must also depend on how much artificial warmth you can give the young plants, and on what time you want the plant to mature. Seeds of the hardier vegetables, for example, such as lettuces, peas, cabbages, can be

harvested earlier than normal if suitable varieties are sown in heat early in the year. In cool climates, seeds of tender and half-hardy vegetables, such as cucumbers, tomatoes, peppers and sweetcorn, all need to be started off in warm conditions indoors as they will produce a limited crop or fail to grow at all.

Temperature for germination

It is a common mistake for beginners to think that the higher the temperature, the better will be the germination of their seed. Too much warmth can, in fact, spoil or even kill the seed.

For most varieties a temperature between 7° and 16°C (45° and 60°F) is perfectly adequate; half-hardy plants, such as begonias, need a temperature at the higher end of this range. For many hardy plants the natural warmth of the soil outdoors or in an unheated greenhouse or frame may be sufficient for germination.

Tender vegetables and fruit, such as tomatoes, sweetcorn, cucumbers, peppers and melons, usually have seeds that need a temperature of about 21°C (70°F) for quick germination. At temperatures lower than this, the seed may rot before it germinates.

For all seeds, too high a temperature forces them to germinate too quickly, and the resulting seedlings become weak, spindly, pale and usually useless.

Propagators

Basically, a propagator is nothing more than a device to provide artifical warmth and to retain the moisture of the compost and the surrounding atmosphere.

Many different types of propagator are available. Some are designed specifically for seed germination, but it is wise to bear in mind that it is most useful if a propagator is large enough to be used for other jobs, such as propagating fruit from cuttings, or for forcing a few pots of strawberries.

Propagators are usually heated by paraffin-oil (kerosene) heaters or by electricity. The latter lends itself to thermostatic control — a highly desirable feature. The simplest type of propagator, designed for seed germination only, may consist merely of a warmed plate on which one or more seed trays can be placed, and a plastic cover which fits over the tray and retains moisture. At the other extreme are large glass or plastic cases with soil- and air-warming electrical cables, and adjustable thermostatic temperature control. With these, you can often find space to return pricked-out or potted seedlings to the case if they need warmth to get them off to a good start. This type of propagator is particularly useful to the greenhouse gardener, or to those interested in tender fruit and vegetables.

An electrically heated propagator with a thermostat is really the best choice, though also the most expensive. A thermostat is useful because the temperature inside the propagator can vary considerably with the temperature of its surroundings. For example, if the greenhouse temperature shoots up during a burst of intense sunshine, a pro-

pagator inside the greenhouse without thermostatic control may 'boil' your seeds.

When buying a propagator, make sure that it is able to maintain the highest temperature you are likely to need; this will be about 24°C (75°F) if you want to use it to germinate the seed of tender plants, fruits and vegetables.

Always site your propagator in a shaded place. If it uses paraffin (kerosene) as the heat source, set the wick to give the lowest temperature necessary and try to check the operation of the propagator as often as possible, especially when the weather is changeable.

Improvising a propagator

In the greenhouse, a section of the staging (benches) can often be used for propagation. It can be covered with moist peat or sand with either electric tubular heaters or a paraffin (kerosene) heater placed below. If the

house is heated by hot-water pipes, a section of the staging can be lowered over them to give a higher local temperature. Again use a maximum and minimum thermometer to check temperatures over a period before risking your seeds. To retain moisture and warmth, the propagation section of the staging can be covered with glass or plastic cloches (Hotkaps), or preferably a glass frame. One of the modern metal frames makes an excellent propagating case.

By using such a frame, you can make a sophisticated general-purpose propagator at a reasonable cost using soil-warming cables. A range of cables is available, having different power ratings. To heat a propagation area of about 0.9 sq m (10 sq ft), a 120 or 150 watt cable is sufficient, and is suitable for the average small garden frame. Full

Commercial nurseries use misting equipment and soil-warming cables.

instructions for laying them are usually issued with the cables.

When you have laid the cables, cover them with about 2.5cm (1in) of sand; *do not use peat* or similar materials, which become good heat insulators when dry and may overheat the cable. You can place your containers of seeds for germination directly on the sand. Always keep the sand moist; the frame will help to do this.

If you have no frame, use cloches or a covering of transparent plastic sheeting to help retain moisture. Sheets of horticultural glass can also be used if they are held together with parent clips or corner pieces cut from thin sheet aluminium with scissors.

To control the temperatures inside your propagator, invest in a rod-type thermostat. Connect this with the warming cable in the same way as a switch, and suspend the thermostat in the air in the propagator by means of suitable supports. Also, it is a good idea to include a small pilot light that glows when the warming cable is on.

If in doubt about the electrical fitting, get a qualified electrician to do the work. Horticultural warming cables and other electrical equipment are specially designed for electrical safety. *Never use domestic electrical equipment*, such as lamps in ordinary bulb-holders, in the greenhouse, in a frame or outdoors.

Containers for sowing

In greenhouses, frames and propagators, seeds are usually sown in containers such as pots and seed-trays. These must be kept very clean, because a good standard of hygiene is essential for successful germination. For this reason, smooth plastic pots are to be preferred to the porous clay types. Plastic pots are extremely light, and are easily stacked so that they can be moved from one place to another or stored in a small space when not in use. Also, they are almost unbreakable, and retain moisture and warmth better than clay pots. If you must use clay pots, you should first sterilize them by boiling them in a saucepan of water for 15 minutes. Small square plastic pots are now obtainable; you

can fit more of them into a propagator than the round type.

Large seeds can usually be individually sown in small pots, particularly if the plants are to be grown on as pot plants. It is more convenient to sow **small seeds** in small plastic trays. These should be preferably square or rectangular, to make the most of the space within your propagator. They need be no more than about 5cm (2in) deep. Wooden seed-trays are best avoided for seed germination, because they can harbour pests and diseases.

It is possible to buy both pots and trays fitted with removable clear plastic domes. These are useful when a covered propagator is not available, or when no extra warmth is needed. In all cases, the containers should have drainage holes in the base in case you overwater. Just as too dry conditions will lead to failure of seeds to germinate, waterlogging is equally harmful, since the seeds must have air as well as moisture. If there are no drainage holes in your plastic containers, you can easily drill some or make them by pushing a heated rod through the base.

In some cases, seeds can be sown directly into 'peat pots' (discs made of a peat-and-fibre mixture, which expand when placed in water to give cylindrical 'pots') or soil blocks (made by compressing a suitable compost with a special machine). The advantage of these is that the entire 'pot' containing a young plant can be transplanted into the soil, thus minimizing damage to the delicate root system. However, these 'pots' are best for potting on seedlings after germination or for the germination of seed needing no propagator treatment.

Seed composts (mixtures)

You should never use garden soil for indoor sowing. It is of the wrong consistency and will probably be full of pests and disease-causing organisms. A seed compost (mixture) should have the ideal texture for seed germination and all the nutrients needed both for germination and to feed the seedlings once they have emerged. It should also be partially sterilized, to kill any weed

seeds, soil pests and disease-causing organisms, but not beneficial soil organisms. It must provide a firm anchorage for the roots of the seedlings, and act as a reservoir for air and water.

Nowadays, many commercial seed composts (mixtures) are available from shops or garden centres. Many are based on peat, but others contain soil as well.

Other composts (mixtures)

Seeds that are large and easy to handle, or those that germinate readily, can be sown direct into a potting compost (mixture) if preferred. The seed will have stored all its needs for germination.

You can use a commercially prepared potting compost (mixture) (which one depends on the plant and the conditions under which it will be grown) or you can make your own potting compost. Mix together equal parts by volume of peat and gritty sand, and to this add a solid, but *soluble*, commercial fertilizer of the balanced type, that is, one containing nitrogen, phosphorus, potassium and preferably some trace elements, in the correct ratio. The label on the container will help in choosing the right kind. You should add about one level teaspoon of the soluble feed and the same amount of powdered chalk to each 12.5cm (5in) potful of the peat/sand mix.

Sowing techniques

To raise plants successfully from seed, whether in containers or out in the garden, start by ensuring conditions of strict hygiene. Inspect all containers, tools, propagators and equipment and make sure that they are thoroughly clean. Check the growing site too; a dirty greenhouse, containing diseased and unhealthy plants, or a messy frame, will simply invite trouble from pests and diseases, leading to poor germination and growth.

Compost (potting mixture) for germinating seed in containers may be a commercial mixture or you might wish to make your own. If mixing your own compost, pay attention to the texture. A mixture containing large pieces of, say, fibrous peat, lumps of loam or sizeable stones, is obviously too coarse. On the other hand, dust-fine compost is undesirable since it will be prone to waterlogging.

If you have a reliable source of sterilized loam (you can sometimes buy it from a nursery), you can easily make your own seed compost (mixture) and save a good deal of money. It is probably worthwhile only if you use a lot of compost; and you need space, preferably outdoors, to mix the ingredients.

Making seed compost (mixture)
To make your own seed compost (mixture) you will need:

2 parts by volume of sterilized loam
1 part by volume of fine, best horticultural peat
1 part by volume of washed clean coarse sand
45g (1½oz) superphosphate per 1.28 cu ft (bushel) of compost
20g (¾oz) powdered chalk of limestone

Mix the loam, peat and sand. To each 1.28 cu ft (bushel) of this mixture add the above amounts of the superphosphate and chalk, and mix thoroughly. A bushel would fill about eight 4 litre (1 gal) household buckets. You will probably not need this much compost, but the more you make the more accurately you will be able to weigh the chemicals. You could join together with friends and neighbours to make such large amounts of compost.

Make sure that the mixture is moist—neither dry nor wet—before using it. You can store it in sealed plastic bags, but use it preferably within about two months of making it. To weigh the chemicals accurately, use small scales designed for those on special diets which are divisible into grams—these can be bought from most large chemists (pharmacies). Any other *very* accurate scale will do as well.

Another reliable seed compost (mixture) is the University of California seed compost (mixture). To make this, mix equal volume of peat and sand. To each 1.28 cu ft (bushel) of this mixture add 15g (½oz) ammonium sulphate, 30g (1oz) superphosphate, 20g (¾oz) potassium sul-

phate, and also 120g (4oz) powdered chalk. The chemicals can be bought from firms specializing in horticultural chemicals, but not usually from an ordinary chemist (pharmacist). Make sure that you do not allow any of them to become damp; keep them in a dry place in a sealed tin or plastic bag.

Aids to germination
For best results, always try to sow seeds as soon as possible after receiving them, or they may lose their ability to germinate.

Seed will germinate only if mois-

Top: peat-based mixtures are easy to buy or can be made up by the gardener. Bottom: wooden boxes are useful for pricked-out seedlings.

ture penetrates it. Some seeds have a hard or thick outer coating and you can speed up germination of these by removing the outer shell. Obviously, only those seeds which are large enough to handle can be treated in this way. Use a suitable tool, such as a sharp razor blade, to take a tiny slice of the coat, or thin the coat by rubbing the seed with sandpaper. When you carry out such operations,

109

make sure that you take great care not to damage the interior of the seed.

Seeds which are too small to handle in this way may be soaked in clean tepid water. Do not soak them for more than a couple of days, however, or the seed may rot. Sometimes you can soak the seed first and remove a piece of the outer shell afterwards. A further germination aid is to soak seed in a two per cent solution of potassium nitrate, a common potash fertilizer.

The seed of some hardy plants, such as fruit and nut-bearing trees and shrubs, may germinate better after exposure to frost. This is called *stratification*. Mix larger seeds with clean moist sand first and leave them in a suitable place outdoors, where they will be protected from rain. Very small seeds can be left in the freezing compartment of a refrigerator, but usually for not more than a month.

Preparing containers

Before sowing, it is vital that the seed compost is thoroughly moist all through, but not waterlogged. You can test the moisture content by squeezing some compost in your hand and then releasing your grip. If the compost stays in a solid lump, it is too wet; if it crumbles apart completely, it is too dry.

Peat-based composts (mixtures) should not be allowed to dry out completely, or they may be difficult to remoisten. If your compost has dried, spread it out on a clean surface and spray with a fine mist of water, turning the compost over as you do. You may have to do this several times, leaving the compost for a few hours between sprayings, before the moisture has penetrated evenly.

Do not fill seed germination trays or pots to the top with compost. In trays, a depth of about 2.5cm (1in) will be adequate. Leave plenty of space for the seedlings to emerge between the compost and the top of the container, since the containers may later be covered with sheets of glass or plastic.

Make sure that the compost is reasonably level and firm, but not compressed. A useful tool for levelling and firming can be made by bending a small rectangle of aluminium sheet to a right angle. One side can be used as a handle and the other for smoothing and gently pressing down the compost.

If you are going to sow fine seed, it is wise to finish with a light covering of seed compost, pressed through a sieve of about ten mesh to 2.5cm (1in). You can make one yourself with a square of wire gauze.

Sowing the seed

To obtain even sowing of very small seed, add some clean, fine silver sand to the seed packet and shake gently. The seed, adhering to the sand, can then be carefully shaken out by tapping the packet with the forefinger. Slightly larger seed can also be sown in this way, but without the addition of sand. Some seed is large enough to be picked up with tweezers, while really large or pelleted seed can be held in the fingers. Flattish seeds, such as those of cucumber, should be sown on their edges.

To protect seed from attack by fungi and pests while germinating, a commercial seed dressing may be used. These dressings usually take the form of powders. A little can be added to the seed in the packet, and the packet shaken to coat the seeds evenly. This treatment is especially useful for outdoor sowing, where a sterile soil is impossible to achieve. It can also be beneficial, however, for indoor sowing of seeds that take a long time to germinate. If treating seed which has been soaked, this should first be spread out on absorbent paper so that surplus moisture evaporates. The coating of pelleted seeds may already contain a pesticidal chemical, so that it is not necessary to give such seeds a dressing.

Every effort should be made not to overcrowd the seeds, because this will make it extremely difficult to transfer seedlings to larger containers, thus increasing the risk of root damage. Care should also be taken not to cover seed too thickly. Generally, very fine seed should not be covered at all, and other seeds covered to their own depth with compost, pressed through a sieve, if necessary. When sowing pelleted seeds outdoors, however, cover them to twice the depth of the greatest dimension. After sowing the seed, lightly sprinkle the surface of the compost or soil with water; never soak it.

Covering the containers

Light can affect the chemical processes which cause germination, so it is important to control the amount.

The best general technique is to cover the containers with translucent sheets of paper, brown or white, topped with sheets of glass or plastic. The glass or plastic will retain moisture, and the paper will protect the seeds from disturbance by condensation, which tends to build up on the undersurface of the glass if no paper is used.

White paper will allow a subdued light to filter through, which will be beneficial to those seeds that germinate better in light. For most vegetable and fruit seeds, however, you will probably get better results by using brown paper instead of white. Algae should not prove to be troublesome if the germination period is two to three weeks, but their growth is almost inevitable during longer periods. They can, however, be held in check if light is kept to a minimum.

Another method for germinating seeds is to slip pots or trays inside polythene or plastic bags. If using a propagator arrangement which includes a case, frame or general cover, you should still cover the seed containers and put the propagator cover in place.

When dealing with unusual seed of foreign fruit and vegetables, the amount of light allowed through may be a critical factor. If in doubt, germinate some of the seed in light and some in dark conditions, covering one group with compost but leaving the rest exposed. You can then be sure that one group of seed will have the right conditions for germination.

Removing coverings

After sowing, daily checks must be made to see that the compost (mixture) is moist and to find out whether germination is taking place. Unless germination time is extra long, compost will usually retain sufficient moisture from sowing time until the seedlings appear, without the addition of extra water. You will find that pelleted seed normally takes a day or two longer to germinate than non-pelleted seed of the same variety.

As soon as the seedlings appear, coverings should be removed at once. The outer coverings of cased-in or covered propagators, however, may be left in place. If germination is patchy, these outer coverings, will retain sufficient moisture for the remaining seed to germinate.

Some propagators have coverings which include vents, which may be opened to let air in if conditions within seem excessively humid and moist. Frame tops can similarly be opened.

Water, air and temperature
In order to germinate, seeds need to be able to 'breathe in' oxygen gas from the air. They also need the correct amount of moisture. Too much water will suffocate the seed

Seeds should be planted in clean trays and clearly labelled.

and will wash water-soluble plant nutrients out of the soil. On the other hand, drying out can cause seeds to die if it occurs just after the roots emerge.

If condensation is excessive, wipe it off the glass each day. When water is required, it is best to use a sprayer with a nozzle adjusted to give a fine mist. Keep the sprayer specially for this job, and do not use it to apply pesticides. Never immerse containers in water, as sometimes suggested, as this will wash out plant nutrients.

Be sure to use only thoroughly clean water, such as drinking water from a tap. Generally, water for seed germination can be either hard or soft. However, for lime-hating plants, it may help to use rainwater. This can be collected by putting out clean bowls just after the rain begins. Store the water in clean, closed containers of plastic or glass.

Most seeds need a higher temperature in which to germinate than that in which the adult plants live. A good level is 15-18°C (60-65°F); this will ensure germination of most seed.

Aftercare
Higher temperatures are necessary only during the germination period, and once germination has occurred, the temperature should be gradually reduced. Generally, seed containers should be moved from the propagator or propagation area to cooler conditions when the seed leaves – the first leaves, round or oval in shape – start to appear.

There are, however, some cases where continued warmth may be helpful. These include delicate plants, greenhouse fruit and vegetables. The seedlings may be left in the propagator until well-established and then moved on to their permanent positions without the danger of a check.

Since seed compost is comparatively limited in plant foods, pricking out into richer potting compost should always be done as soon as possible. It is usually best to do this before the first true leaf appears. Seedlings awaiting pricking out should be shaded from direct sunlight and protected from chill or excessive warmth. Light is needed, though, to keep them sturdy and green. Seed-

lings which would benefit from continued warmth can be pricked out into potting compost and then returned to the propagator.

Thinning out
Unless the seed was large enough to be spaced out correctly when sowing, the resulting seedlings will need to be thinned out or the plants, when fully grown, will be overcrowded. To minimize soil disturbance and plant damage, unwanted seedlings should be removed when about 1cm (½in) tall. The operation will also be made easier if the soil is watered with a fine spray on the morning before the work is to take place. Thinning must be carried out twice, particularly in the case of root vegetables such as carrots and parsnips. Several weeks should elapse between thinnings.

The disturbance of some seedlings, such as those of onion and carrot, will increase their natural aroma and may thus attract pests. Remove any thinnings left lying around, and firm the soil to discourage pests from burrowing down and laying their eggs on the roots and bases of the plants.

Seedling troubles
Damping off is a disease caused by several fungi. Affected seedlings rot at the base and topple over. The use of sterilized compost (potting mixture) and general cleanliness will almost eliminate the risk of damping off, at least in the early stages. Since the spores of the fungi can be airborne, they may reach older seedlings after pricking out.

Various fungicides, such as Cheshunt compound, are made specifically to control damping-off disease. They are usually best applied after pricking out; alternatively, apply them to the compost before sowing the seed.

Another seedling trouble, producing similar effects to damping off, is attack by the maggots of the *sciarid fly*. These infest the roots and bases of the plants. Close inspection of the compost (mixture) even scraping the surface if necessary, will reveal the whitish, worm-like maggots, 2-3mm (⅛in) in length. Keep an eye open also for the gnat-like flies. With severe

infestations, there may be a trace of slime on the compost surface.

The flies themselves can be killed with most general insecticidal sprays, but the maggots are remarkably resistant to treatment. Sciarid fly is especially troublesome with peat-based compost (mixture). Stale or wet peat, long exposed to the air, may be a harbouring place for the maggots. The best prevention is to cover seed trays and all peat or compost in store, and to use only fresh peat for making compost.

Cultivating successful seedlings
Once your seedlings have germinated and formed their roots, they will reach only a limited stage of development in their seed compost (mixture) —they now need different combinations and concentrations of plant foods. The next stage, then, in the

With careful planning a small greenhouse can hold many seedlings.

care of your seedlings is 'pricking out', moving them on to a new place of growth in potting compost or soil.

Pricking out
The more carefully you sow seed to avoid overcrowding the easier pricking out will be. Nevertheless it is still one of the more delicate horticultural operations that has to be faced by most gardeners.

Although you might think that pricking out would be easier if you waited for seedlings to reach an appreciable size, it has been found that far fewer failures result if it is done as soon as possible. Less damage is done to the roots and the seedlings grow up far more quickly in the potting compost (mixture). The smaller

112

the seedlings, the more difficult pricking out can be, but many popular fruits and vegetables like tomatoes, cucumbers, peas, beans, sweet corn or sweet .peppers, which have relatively large seeds, should present no difficulty at all. Their seedlings are usually large, too, and quite easy to handle.

The best time to prick out is when the first seed leaves are fully formed, but *before* any true leaves (having the characteristic shape of the mature plant foliage) have formed. With those seedlings, such as those of melons, which have large seed leaves, you can often use one leaf as a 'handle' during the pricking-out procedure, if you hold it carefully between finger and thumb. With more delicate seedlings, you may need one or two tools for pricking out.

Home made tools for pricking out
You can easily make a few very simple tools to lift the seedlings from the place where they have germinated to their new home. Take a few strips of wood, plastic, or sheet aluminium 0.5–1.5 cm ($\frac{1}{5}$–$\frac{3}{5}$ in) wide and cut V-shaped notches in their ends. The 'prongs' of different sizes so formed can be used to lift the seedlings from their·containers, and you can then choose a pricking-out tool of suitable size for the size of the seedlings being dealt with.

Alternatively, a useful tool is a pair of long and finely-tipped tweezers; these can be bought from most surgical shops or large chemists (pharmacies). One pair of tweezers, depending on how closely they are pressed together, can usually be used for a wide range of seedling sizes. The same tool is also useful for handling small seeds when sowing.

Pricking out technique
Usually both hands should be used to prick out seedlings. Normally the pricking-out tool will be held in the left hand so that its prongs gently grip the stem of the seedling beneath the seed-leaves. During lifting and transferring, the seedling can be held in place on the tool by holding one of the seed leaves very gently between the finger and thumb of the left hand. With modern composts (mixtures) containing peat, very little root damage should result. The delicate roots penetrate peat fibres as the seed germinates and the fibres come away easily with the roots when the seedlings are transferred.

Thinning
If the seedlings are very crowded, it often helps to thin them before pricking out. This is done by pulling out and discarding surplus seedlings to create some room around others. Obviously this is a wasteful practice, but it can be done at little cost with very cheap seed. Thinning is also a common procedure for outdoor sowing.

Spacing and siting
Obviously you should make your preparations for the growing on of the seedlings before you start pricking them out. Larger seedlings can be transferred to small pots for growing on in frames or in the greenhouse depending on the amount of warmth they require. Some tender plants need to be grown permanently in the greenhouse, or to be put outdoors only after all danger of frost has passed. More hardy vegetables like cauliflower and other brassicas can usually be given frame protection, and often the seedlings can be accommodated in seed trays. If any seedlings are to be grown on in quantity seed trays may also be more convenient than pots.

For many vegetables and fruits to be grown outdoors later, pricking out into peat pots, fibre pots or soil blocks may be preferable. These kinds of container are not removed when planting out since they rot down in the soil, incidentally providing humus for the plants. This speeds planting and avoids late root disturbance. Some peat pots are sold in the form of discs that have to be immersed in water, when they swell to form pots. They contain fertilizer added to the peat to feed the young plants.

Before placing the pricked-out seedlings in the potting compost, make a depression large enough to accommodate the roots. Use your index finger or, for small seedlings, the end of a pencil to make the depressions. You need then only gently cover the roots with potting compost pushed in from around each depression, using the fingers or the flat end of the pricking-out tool. Make sure that the roots of the seedlings are covered and put them in at such a depth that the seed comes just above the surface. A seedling which has a lot of stem showing after pricking out becomes a drawn and straggly plant, or dies. Press each seedling in to make sure it is firm— but do not press it too hard. You may have to adjust the position or re-firm the seedling after watering. For several days after pricking them out, shade the seedlings from strong sunlight until they resume growth, and reduce the amount of ventilation.

The spacing of seedlings in seed trays is most important. When you grow your own, you can be generous with the space given to each seedling. This will greatly help the plants by providing more potting compost (mixture) for each one and making dividing up much easier when planting out later. Often when buying seedlings, the seedlings are so crushed together that when separating them each ends up with severely damaged, weak roots with hardly any compost adhering to them. How much space you give to your seedlings will depend on the size they are expected to reach. For the standard seed tray with a surface area of about 36×22cm ($14 \times 8\frac{1}{2}$in) about 24 seedlings is a rough recommended number; make sure they are evenly spaced.

Potting composts (mixtures)
All seedlings moved to trays or pots should be given a properly formulated potting compost. Potting composts contain longer-acting fertilizers than seed composts—enough to take the plants to an advanced stage when they are ready for planting in larger pots or other containers, greenhouse borders, or outdoors.

As with the seed composts, there are numerous ready-mixed commercial types that you can buy from most garden shops, garden centres or nurseries.

One reliable compost is the soil-less University of California potting compost mixture. You can make your own potting composts but, as with seed composts, this is worthwhile only if you use large amounts or can share it with neighbours or friends.

Grow-bags

For growing popular crops under glass, such as tomatoes, cucumbers and melons, there are plastic sacks, containing specially-prepared compost, called 'grow-bags'. These are placed on their side, holes are cut in the uppermost side, according to the manufacturer's instructions, and the plants—usually two to four to each bag—set in the compost. These bags can of course also be used for outdoor growing if desired. When grow-bags are used, the plants are then grown on to the harvesting stage without any further potting-on or moving.

After care of seedlings

Extra precautions against 'damping off' are specially important after pricking out. As a routine measure it is wise to water-in all seedlings with Cheshunt Compound, a copper-based fungicide. This can be bought as crystals and should be dissolved in water and diluted—preferably with *clean* rainwater—as directed on the label. The solution should be applied with a fine spray so as to thoroughly wet the seedlings and moisten the potting compost—but not so thoroughly that it causes water-logging.

A very modern and useful treatment for seedlings is to spray them from an early stage with a foliar feed containing vitamins and plant growth hormones. The vitamins and hormones accelerate root formation and establishment of the seedlings, and also seem to aid disease resistance. For some plants a very dramatic improvement is found compared with untreated seedlings, and spraying with the feed at intervals can be continued almost to the cropping stage. All root crops benefit particularly.

All seedlings need a position with good light, but in frames and greenhouses do not put them too near the glass at first. It is a common mistake to think that the nearer seedlings are to the glass the better. Provided the frame or greenhouse is not cluttered and overshadowed, the seedlings may well be safer on the staging or even underneath if the greenhouse is glazed right down to the ground. Seedlings on shelves near the glass or up near the roof may well get frosted or suffer from cold during the earlier months of the year, and it is a fallacy to suppose that the light there will be any more intense than it is on the staging.

Hardening-off

The term 'hardening-off' means getting plants and seedlings ready for their permanent positions outdoors where they will be fully exposed to the weather. Plants suddenly transferred from the congenial atmosphere of a greenhouse or frame where it may be warm, humid and slightly shaded, to the night chill, direct day sunshine, and wind, of the open air, may be severely checked. Foliage may shrivel and growth cease for some time. All the benefits of earlier cultivation under cover will then be lost and your time wasted.

Careful hardening-off is particularly important for those seedlings raised early in the year that are to be planted out from spring onwards. Take special care with frost-tender plants, such as tomatoes, marrows (squash), outdoor (ridge) cucumbers, sweet corn, sweet peppers and cape gooseberries and of aubergines (egg-plants). Some degree of hardening-off is necessary for these plants even if they are to be grown on under glass outdoors or in a cool greenhouse until harvesting time. In this case, after pricking out, they should be *gradually* moved to the coolest part of the greenhouse. Extend this over a week or so.

In the case of plants for outdoors, allow a three to four week period for hardening off. First treat the seedlings as if they were to be grown on under glass by moving them to the coolest part of the greenhouse. After this, an outdoor frame is really essential. Portable frames are extremely useful, since they can be first sited in a sheltered shady place and later moved to a fully open position. The seedlings must also be protected from direct sunshine at first. You can shade the frames with an electro-static shading paint which wipes off easily but will not wash off with the occasional shower. Keep the frames closed at night and, while it is cold, during the day as well. Gradually increase the ventilation and exposure to light until the frame tops are left off and the plants are fully exposed.

The process of hardening-off should begin three to four weeks before you can expect to plant out the seedlings. This will vary with the hardiness of the plants, the time of year when you want the crop to mature, or, very often, when you expect the danger of frost to pass. Much will depend on the local climate where you live.

All the time the plants are in the frames be careful to keep them watered—they may dry out more quickly than in the open—and watch out for pests like greenfly.

Planting out and aftercare

The planting-out site should have been prepared well in advance by digging, weeding and incorporating garden compost, manures, and fertilizers. Try to choose a day when the soil is moist, but neither dry nor wet, and the weather is good enough for you to do the job at your own speed and comfort.

Most fruit and vegetables are best set in rows, orientated in an east-west direction so that each plant benefits from winter sunlight. Try to make the rows and the plant distances even and allow enough room for you to walk about to weed and cultivate. The best distances to leave between rows and plants will vary depending on the particular vegetable or variety and on the expected ultimate size of the plants. Positioning the plants is much easier if you use marked sticks and strings stretched across the plot, especially for larger areas. Rake over the site to level the surface and use a hand trowel or a dibber (dibble) to make holes to take the plant roots.

Plants in a pot can be removed with the soil ball around their roots intact by inverting the pots, allowing the stem to pass between the fingers, and tapping the rim of the pot sharply with the trowel handle. If you are planting out in a greenhouse border or frame, you can tap the rim of the pot on the staging (benches) or side of the frame.

Plants in plastic seed trays usually come away easily with their soil balls if the tray is set carefully on its side and tapped gently. Be careful with old plastic trays—they can become brittle and may crack. With wooden trays, a side can be removed by levering off with an old screwdriver or other suitable tool.

All plants must be watered to moisten them thoroughly before planting and the soil site should also be moist. This is particularly important when peat-pots or similar containers are used, which are planted together with the plants. In dry conditions peat pots may not rot down to free the roots as intended.

After planting, gently press in the soil around the roots to firm them, but do not compress it so much that you damage them. 'Water in' each plant carefully. Later watering can include some weak, balanced liquid fertilizer or a foliar feed with hormones and vitamins as described for pricking out. In some cases the plants can be covered by cloches (Hotkaps) for a time to protect them from cold weather or damage by birds.

Vegetative propagation

Although growing plants from seed in your greenhouse, frame or cloche is satisfying and cheap, it is still quicker to raise particular plants by vegetative propagation, that is by cuttings, layering and division.

Cuttings

There are various different types of cuttings which are widely used for propagation purposes. The parts of a plant used may consist of young, green stem-growths, semi-ripe wood, hard-wood, single leaves, buds and roots.

Stem cuttings These can be taken 7.5cm-10cm (3-4in) in length or half-ripe shoots in July or August of such plants as cistus, hydrangeas, hebes and the like. Some, such as those of camellias, may have a heel of the old wood attached ('heel' cuttings),

though most cuttings are prepared by trimming them just below a node or joint ('nodal' cuttings) with a sharp knife or razor blade. The cuttings should be inserted to about a quarter of their depth in pots of moist sandy soil, or a reliable cutting compost (mixture), or a mixture of sand and peat, or in a sandy propagating bed in a cold frame. Such cuttings should be shaded from direct sunlight and be lightly sprayed over with tepid water each morning until roots have formed. Any cuttings that show signs of damping off should be removed.

Soft stem cuttings In the spring young shoots may be taken from the base of such plants as chrysanthemums and dahlias which have been brought into early growth in a warm greenhouse or frame. These are known as soft stem cuttings and after they have been prepared by

trimming them cleanly below a node or joint and removing the lower leaves, they should be inserted to a quarter of their depth in moist, sandy soil in a propagating frame with a temperature of about 13°C (55°F). Delphiniums, lupins, heleniums and many other plants, such as the somewhat tender lemon-scented verbena (*Lippia citriodora*), may be treated in this manner. Cuttings of the more tender plants such as dahlias may be rooted more quickly if the propagating frame is supplied with bottom heat and a very moist atmosphere is maintained, by inserting the cuttings in pots of moist sand or other rooting mixture, and plunging the pots in moist peat in the frame, and spraying them overhead each day. However, as far as the hardier plants, such as lupins and delphiniums are concerned, too much heat and too moist an atmo-

Hydrangea cuttings are made from short noded non-flowering shoots.

Trim and make a straight cut immediately below a node.

Dibble in the cuttings around the edge of a small pot.

Several cuttings can be put into each pot.

sphere may easily result in the loss of cuttings through damping-off disease or other fungus diseases. Once such soft stem cuttings have rooted they should be potted singly, or, in some instances they may be planted out in the open, provided they are not neglected. They should be protected from direct sunlight and drying winds while they are becoming established.

Leaf cuttings Healthy, well-developed leaves of numerous plants provide a useful means of propagation. Those that root particularly easily by this means include various begonias, such as *Begonia rex*, gloxinias, saintpaulias, streptocarpus, and some ferns, both tender and hardy. After removing a leaf from the parent plant make a few light incisions with a sharp knife across the veins on the underside and then lay the leaf on the surface of moist compost (mixture) consisting of peat and sharp sand. Peg the leaf down gently; hairpins are useful for this purpose. Leaf cuttings should be shaded from direct sunlight and have a reasonably warm and moist atmosphere. Begonia leaves, among others, will produce quite quickly,

1. *A well-secured plastic bag helps maintain a humid atmosphere.*
2. *Soft cuttings of chrysanthemums are taken in winter.*
3. *Soft cuttings of coleus are taken from non-flowering shoots.*
4. *Cuttings are trimmed below a joint.*
5. *Cuttings are put in sandy compost.*

even when just placed in a saucer of water, but the difficulty is that the roots are so tender that potting on the young plantlets is quite a problem.

Camellias are frequently increased by means of leaf-bud cuttings, which are similar, except the leaf is taken from the current year's growth, complete with a plump, dormant bud with a small piece of stem wood attached. Such leaves are inserted in sharp, moist sand in pots or in a propagating frame in March in gentle heat. With the aid of moist propagation it is possible to deal with much larger numbers of cuttings over a longer period and the percentage that root is usually greater.

Rooting cuttings in polythene film
An interesting way of rooting hardwood or semi-hardwood cuttings without inserting them in the normal rooting compost (mixture), is to use polythene film or thin plastic sheeting. The cuttings are prepared in the normal manner and a piece of film about 20-23cm (8-9in) wide and, say, 45cm (18in) long, is placed on the propagating bench. On one half of this, along the length, is placed a layer of damp sphagnum moss. The cuttings are then placed on this (their bases may first be dipped in hormone rooting powder if desired) about 6-25mm (½-1in) apart, their tops projecting over the edge of the polythene strip. The lower half of the strip of film is then folded up over the moss and the cuttings. Then, starting at one end and working towards the other, the strip of film with the moss and cuttings is rolled up tightly and tied top and bottom with raffia or fillis. Roots should eventually form and these will be visible through the clear polythene. When all or most of the cuttings have rooted the roll can be untied and the cuttings potted up or planted out, taking care not to break the brittle young roots. Damage to the roots may prove fatal.

The advantages of this method are that once the roll has been tied up no further watering is needed as moisture will not evaporate through the

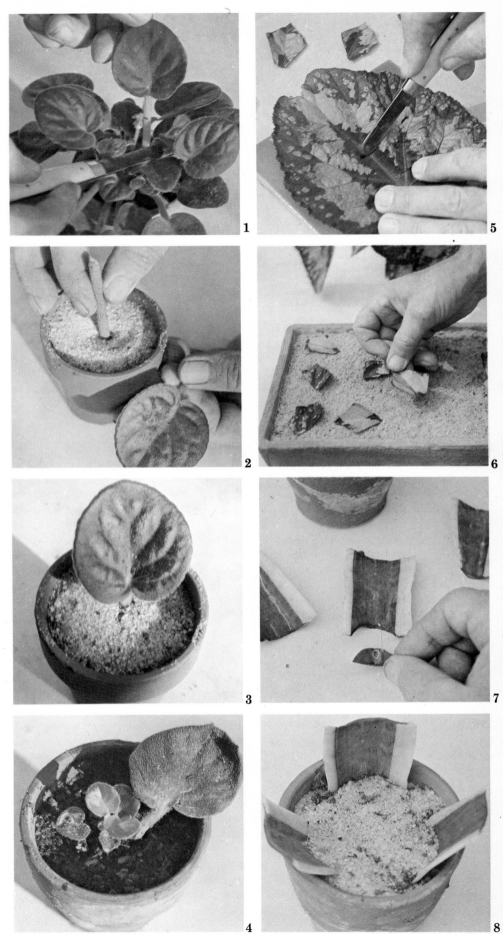

1. African violets are easy to grow from leaf cuttings.
2. Use a small pot and sandy mixture.
3 & 4. New shoots will form quickly.
5 & 6. Begonia rex leaves, if cut up and placed on damp sand will root.
7 & 8. Sansevieria can be propagated from trimmed sections placed round the edge of a pot with sandy compost.

film (the roll should, however, be kept out of direct sunshine, on the greenhouse shelf or bench, even on a window sill), and that a number of cuttings can be rooted in a quite small space.

Hygiene

When preparing cuttings, particularly soft stem cuttings which are liable to be attacked by soil-borne diseases or by virus diseases transmitted by insect vectors, it is advisable to take precautions against such attacks. Always use a clean razor blade or knife, if necessary sterilizing the blade in a sterilant or disinfectant. When a batch of cuttings of, say, dahlias or chrysanthemums is being prepared for rooting it is essential to ensure that they do not flag while they are waiting to be inserted in the compost. As soon as each cutting has been taken from the chrysanthemum stool or dahlia tuber, drop it in a container of aired water to which a few drops of disinfectant has been added.

Virus diseases may be transmitted by sucking pests such as aphids. For this reason, when quantities of cuttings are to be rooted, it is advisable to fumigate the greenhouse beforehand and also to spray stools and tubers with a suitable insecticide and to dip cuttings in an inseticidal solution before they are rooted. Trouble with damping-off diseases can be prevented by watering the cutting compost (mixture) with Cheshunt Compound. This is less necessary with pure sand or sand/ peat mixtures as both these should be reasonably sterile.

Mist propagation

Modern electrically controlled mist propagation units are fitted with jets that emit a fine spray to envelop cuttings with moisture in order to raise the relative humidity. This used to be done with the aid of a hand syringe but it is much more accurately carried out by the 'electronic leaf' which is placed among the cuttings. As soon as the 'leaf' becomes dry the spray is turned on for a predetermined period. Cuttings inserted in a sandy propagating bed heated by electric soil-warming cables will root more quickly than in a cold frame, and with a mist unit installed it is not necessary to shade cuttings, except during very hot, sunny weather.

Soft stem cuttings rooted under mist must be potted at an early stage and grown on in a greenhouse before being hardened off. Semi-hardwood cuttings can be left in the mist for a longer period as they do not usually make so much top growth, and hardwood cuttings can remain in the cutting bed until the spring, if necessary. Mist propagation is not the answer to all the problems of rooting cuttings, but it is particularly useful with large-leaved evergreens, such as camellias, and it has also proved successful with acers (maples), large-flowered clematis hybrids, various conifers, dahlias, daphnes, hibiscus, ilex (holly), magnolias, mahonias, pittosporums, pyracanthas, rhododendrons, azaleas (lilacs), syringas and viburnums, as can be seen in commercial nurseries.

Rooting compounds

Chemical substances, known as rooting hormones, are available both in liquid and powder form, and are useful for accelerating the rooting of cuttings that may otherwise prove difficult. They are not the answer to the rooting of all types of cuttings, but when used according to the manufacturer's instructions can prove to be a valuable aid. With the powder the cutting is prepared and then the base is dipped into the powder before being inserted in the rooting compost (mixture). When using the liquid formulations the prepared cuttings are stood in a container, filled to a depth of about 2.5-5cm (1-2in), for some hours before being inserted in the rooting compost (mixture).

The actual substances are used in minute quantities. For instance, one of them, naphthoxyacetic acid is used at the rates of between 2 parts and 25 parts per million. Three other substances, alpha-naphthalene-acetic acid, indolylbutric acid and beta-indolyl-acetic acid, are used at rates ranging from 10-200 parts per million, depending on the type of cutting which is being rooted.

Layering

Layering is the increasing of an established plant by means of pegging down a long healthy shoot to the ground after making a short cut through a joint (or node), so that the plant will root from this area into the earth. Although not a common method of propagation in the greenhouse, it is particularly useful when applied to the increase of plants such as *Hoya carnosa* and *Laperia rosea*. During spring or summer, peg the strong growths into small pots filled with a reliable potting compost (mixture) and leave to root and form new plants. When the new plant is established, sever it from the parent plant and transplant or pot on as necessary.

Air layering Air layering is the method of propagating plants of habit whose shoots cannot be bent down to the ground, so the ground must be taken to the shoot. The basic principles are the same as for layering but, instead of potting compost, sphagnum moss is used as the rooting medium. Another difference is that a complete ring is cut around the shoot with a sharp knife about 23cm (9in) from the apex and a generous handful of damp sphagnum moss is placed all round the wound, after any leaves on this part of the stem have been removed, but not those at the tip. The moss is kept in place with a piece of polythene; preferably black polythene used in a double layer. This is then carefully tied top and bottom to form a neat little bundle. Healthy, young, pencil-thick shoots should be chosen for air-layering, not old, hardwood.

As with layering, spring and summer are the best times for this operation. When roots are to be seen in the moss, the layer should be severed from the parent and the young plant very carefully potted in an appropriate soil compost (mixture). This is tricky, for at this stage the roots are tender and easily broken, and they will require careful attention and nursing. Careful shading from direct sun and daily spraying with tepid water will assist them at this period, either in a cold frame or a cold greenhouse. Certain greenhouse plants may be propagated in this way, particularly *Ficus elastica*, the India-rubber plant, and these will require much warmer conditions when they are being grown on. The time for an air layer to make roots varies considerably with the plant, in some instances it may be many months, though the time may be reduced by the sprinkling of hormone rooting powder (see page 118) around the cut on the stem before damp moss is placed around it.

Division

Division is a method of propagation in which a plant is separated into two or more parts, each complete with roots and growth buds. Division should be done either in spring, when the plants are just starting into growth, or in autumn, when the plants are dormant. The divided parts should generally be planted immediately. In the greenhouse, division is used particularly to increase plants such as arums, orchids, ferns and marantas. Established plants are taken from their pots and the old compost removed. Then, using a sharp knife or your fingers, divide the plant and re-pot.

When dividing orchids such as cymbidiums, cattleyas, and miltonias, remember that this is a major operation and some care and attention is necessary so far as watering and shading are concerned, until they have developed a good new root system to sustain themselves.

Vine eyes

Grapevines are increased by the removal and planting of 'eyes', pieces of dormant one-year vine rods or stems, each with a plump bud in the autumn. These stem cuttings should be about 4cm (1½in) in length. With the aid of a sharp knife, remove a strip of wood 3mm (⅛in) thick from the wood behind the bud to encourage root formation. The pieces of stem should then be placed horizontally, with the bud uppermost, on the surface of individual pots containing sandy soil and pegged down with pieces of bent wire. Place them in a propagating frame with a bottom heat of 24°C (75°F) and keep moist. When roots have formed and top growth is evident, the pieces should be potted separately and grown on under glass in a temperature of about 16°C (60°F).

1. To air layer Ficus elastica, *first tie the top leaves out of the way.*
2 & 3. Remove leaves on a section of stem and make a slanting cut.
4 & 5. Insert damp sphagnum into the cut and bind it around the stem.
6 & 7. Cover with plastic film.

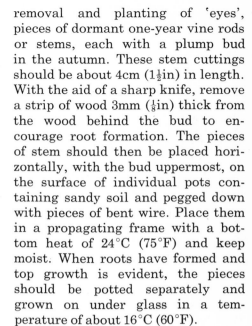

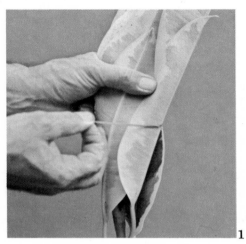

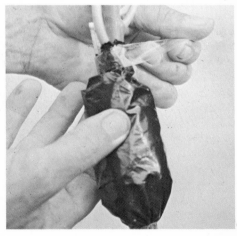

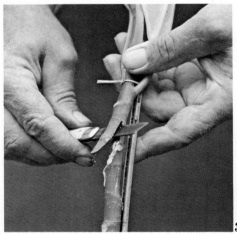

Greenhouse gardener's diary

January

Because space is limited, valuable and expensive to heat in the greenhouse, the propagating case or even cold frames, it is important to plan ahead so that it is usefully occupied. So make a list in January of all the plants you wish to grow and the seeds you wish to germinate, together with their quantities; otherwise you may find yourself heating expensive air, or, worse still, without space or facilities for plants or seedlings requiring the protection or aid given by a greenhouse, propagator or frame.

Remove dead flowers and fading leaves and take care never to over-

Above: mixed polyanthus.
Opposite: hippeastrums, often called amaryllis, are bulbous plants.

water. Any mildewed or diseased plants or cuttings should also be removed before they infect healthy plants. Take cuttings of chrysanthemums. Sow seeds of lilies, *Begonia semperflorens* and sweet peas.

February

If a temperature of about 10°C (50°F) can be maintained in the greenhouse or propagating frame, some of the summer bedding plants, invaluable for a colourful display, can be sown now.

In addition to *Begonia semperflorens*, the sowing of antirrhinums, lobelia, ageratum and *Salvia splendens*, can now take place. But note that *Salvia splendens* needs a higher temperature, of at least 16°C (60°F) and it should not be sown until this can be maintained.

Sow the seeds in a recommended seed compost (mixture) made firm and level in well-drained pots or boxes, with the seed covered to about twice its depth except in the case of very tiny seeds, which should be merely pressed into the surface. After sowing, soak the boxes or pots

Above: snowdrops can make attractive alpine house plants, as do a large number of smaller bulbous plants, such as dwarf iris and narcissi.

from underneath until the moisture seeps through to the surface. Then cover them with glass and paper. Turn the glass daily to remove condensation and never let the compost become dry.

For a more unusual display, cannas may be used in mild, sunny areas. They will make very showy pot-plants. To avoid root disturbance later on, the large black seeds are best sown singly 2.5cm (1in) deep in 7.5cm (3in) pots of an appropriate potting compost (mixture) after the hard outer covering has first been filed through or the seeds soaked in warm water for 24 hours. A temperature of at least 21°C (70°F) is needed for good germination but a slightly lower temperature will do for dormant canna roots, which may be bought now and boxed up in moist peat or leafmould.

For a colourful greenhouse display sow *Primula obconica*, celosias ('cockscombs'), tuberous begonias, gloxinias and the 'Christmas Cherry' (*Solanum capsicastrum*). A temperature of 16°C (60°F) will do for most of these seeds but gloxinias need a temperature of at least 18-21°C (65-70°F). So if this temperature cannot be maintained yet, leave the gloxinias until next month.

For 'home-grown' tomatoes, seed should also be sown now, 6mm (¼in) deep and 2.5cm (1in) apart in potting compost in at least a temperature of 16°C (60°F). But much cooler conditions will do for such vegetables as Brussels sprouts, cauliflowers, cabbages, leeks, lettuce and onions, all of which may be sown in boxes or pots for planting out later.

Dormant plants stored through the winter should also be started off now. If zonal pelargoniums ('geraniums') have been stored close together in boxes, pot them up singly in potting compost. When they start to grow, cut them back to about 15cm (6in) high.

To start fuchsias into growth cut them well back before increasing the water supply and keeping them well syringed. But on no account must hydrangeas be cut back now or there will be no blooms. Stand these in full light and give them more water gradually.

Other dormant plants that may also be started now are gloxinias, tuberous begonias and hippeastrums. Bed the tubers of the first two close together in boxes of moist peat or leafmould so that their tops (the concave side) are just visible. Then keep them just moist at a temperature of 13°C (55°F) for begonias and 18°C (65°F) for gloxinias. Hippeastrums need repotting only every three or four years and until then all they need is the renewal of the top 2.5cm (1in) of compost (soil mixture). When this has been done, cut off any remaining leaves from the plants before keeping them almost dry in plenty of warmth.

When cuttings of the large chrysanthemums taken last month are making obvious growth, pot them up singly into 7.5cm (3in) pots of potting compost burying as little of the actual stem as possible. Cuttings of the reflexed and incurved decorative varieties may also be taken now, together with those of the early-flowering outdoor varieties. Use basal shoots about 5cm (2in) long, insert them firmly in boxes of potting compost and after a thorough soaking allow them to become practically dry before soaking them again.

Perpetual carnation cuttings may still be taken up to mid-February, using young shoots about 10cm (4in) long from about half way up the plant. After trimming these off beneath a joint remove the leaves from the bottom 2.5cm (1in) of stem, then dibble the cuttings 18mm (¾in) deep in clean sand or vermiculite in a propagating frame at a temperature of about 10°C (50°F).

Cuttings rooted earlier should be potted into 7.5cm (3in) pots of potting compost (mixture) with only their roots firmly covered. To get them quickly on the move again a temperature of about 13°C (55°F) is needed.

For a spring display in the cold greenhouse, pot up a few wallflowers, forget-me-nots, polyanthuses and primroses in ordinary soil with some sharp sand for drainage. Ample ventilation is needed for these.

Opposite: the handsome leaves of bromeliads make them striking plants.

March

There is still time to sow the summer bedding plants mentioned in the notes under February. If desired, to these may now be added alyssum, nemesia, stocks, asters, *Mesembryanthemum criniflorum*, French and African marigolds, petunias, kochias, *Phlox drummondii* and cosmeas. All should be sown in the same way as the earlier ones. In cold greenhouses sowing should take place preferably towards the end of the month.

Tuberous begonias, gloxinias, celosias, *Primula obconica* and *Solanum capsicastrum* may also still be sown as in February with, in addition, the beautiful schizanthus or poor man's orchid, as it is sometimes called, easily raised from seed to flower in summer in cool airy conditions.

As the winter-flowering pot plants come to an end, *Azalea indica*, cyclamens and *Solanum capsicastrum* can be kept for next year; but cinerarias and calceolarias are best discarded. Trim the faded flowers off the azaleas, then keep the plants well watered and syringed in the greenhouse to induce new growth.

Cyclamens need gradually less water until they die down, while the solanums should be cut back to about 15cm (6in) high and repotted into pots one size larger, using suitable potting compost plus a pinch of Epsom salts (magnesium sulphate).

Tomatoes may still be sown as in February but where earlier-sown ones have already made their seed leaves (the first pair formed) these will be ready for pricking out.

Bedding plants and pot plants sown earlier will also need pricking out as soon as they are large enough to handle, in most cases at about 6mm ($\frac{1}{4}$in) high.

This pricking out needs care, particularly with tomatoes. Use clean, well-drained seed boxes almost filled to the rim with potting compost (mixture) made firm and level. Use a small fork or trowel to lift the seedlings out of the seed compost, making sure that they are moist beforehand. Then dibble them firmly into the new compost at about 4cm ($\frac{1}{2}$in) apart.

Handle the seedlings by the leaves, not the stem, and bury those with an obvious stem right up to the seed leaves; the others should only 'sit' on the surface, with their roots well anchored.

The dormant plants mentioned in the February notes may still be started into growth, but where this has already been done cuttings should be taken as they become visible. For zonal pelargoniums use young shoots about 10cm (4in) long, trimmed off beneath a joint. These should be inserted about 2.5cm (1in) deep in potting compost or in clean sand or vermiculite, in warm, airy, conditions in full light.

For fuchsia cuttings use young shoots about 5cm (2in) long. Remove the leaves from the lower 2.5cm (1in) of stem before inserting the cuttings in the same way as the zonal pelargoniums but preferably in a propagating frame — although they can be rooted more slowly on the open greenhouse bench in gentle heat.

If any fuchsia cuttings were rooted last summer, a few of these can be grown on as 'standards' by removing all the side shoots (but not the leaves) from the main stem until this reaches the height that is required.

Gloxinias and tuberous begonias may also still be started into growth. But where those started earlier have already made 2.5-5cm (1-2in) of growth, pot them up singly in well-drained 7.5cm (3in) pots of potting compost.

Water them sparingly until growth starts again, which should soon be seen to take place if the begonias are kept at a temperature of about 10°C (50°F) and the gloxinias at 15°C (60°F).

With the coming of March, cacti need more water. So give them a thorough soaking to start them off. If their growth, including the spines, has reached the sides of the pot they should then be transferred in pots a size larger, using an appropriate potting compost (mixture) mixed with a sixth part of sharp sand grit and crushed brick to provide drainage.

If a little heat is available, dahlias can be started early in the month by standing them upright in boxes and working some light, peaty soil in among them until only the tops of the actual tubers are visible. Do not bury the base of the stem. If the soil is kept just moist there should soon be plenty of shoots to use as cuttings.

Continue to take cuttings of decorative and early-flowering chrysanthemums and to pot up those that are already rooted. After potting make sure that they get ample light and ventilation; this is essential to ensure strong, sturdy plants.

Cuttings of perpetual carnations should be potted up as they become rooted, while those that have already nearly filled the 7.5cm (3in) pots with roots should be moved on into 15cm (6in) ones, using an appropriate potting compost (mixture) over perfect drainage. Maximum light and air must be given to these plants now, with only enough heat to keep them safe from frost.

Climbing plants are not advisable inhabitants in greenhouses devoted to tomatoes, chrysanthemums or carnations but otherwise they make most attractive features. *Hoya carnosa*, wax flower; *Plumbago capensis*, cape lead wort; *Passiflora caerulea*, passion flower; and *Stephanotis floribunda* are all fine ones to grow in pots. Use a rough, peaty compost for the *Hoya carnosa* and a more appropriate potting compost for the others. For the *Stephanotis floribunda* try to keep the temperature above 10°C (50°F) but the others need only to be safe from frost. Established plants of the passion flower should be thinned out and cut well back now.

Cinerarias come in many colours. Opposite: camellias flower early.

124

April

April sees much faster growth in the plants in the greenhouse so make sure that all of them, including cacti, get increasingly more water now. If possible, water them in the morning so that they are not wet and cold by night. In very hot weather avoid a dry atmosphere by wetting the floor and staging ('damping down') during the day.

Perpetual carnations in particular need frequent syringeing in hot weather, while those just coming into bud in cold greenhouses should be disbudded by removing all but the main central bud at the tip of each main stem.

Further sowings of summer bedding plants may be made now without artificial heat but they should be treated in the same way as the February and March ones, which must be pricked out as they become ready. Towards the end of April, a sowing of zinnias may also be made in boxes or pots to provide plants for bedding or cutting. The much hardier antirrhinums, already sown and pricked out, can go into a cold frame, with plenty of air during the day and protection from frost at night.

If the frames are already occupied with pansies or violas these may be safely planted out after they have first been hardened off.

Fuchsia and geranium cuttings can still be taken, while those rooted earlier will need potting up into 8cm (3½in) pots of potting compost (mixture). Geraniums need all the sunshine they can get but fuchsias are better in light shade on hot days. Fuchsias will need stopping at about 15cm (6in) high if they have not already branched out.

Solanum capsicastrum, the Christmas cherry, is another plant that needs stopping — by pinching the young plants back to about 5cm (2in) high when they have made 7.5-10cm (3-4in) growth. Some growers also stop the schizanthus, an operation which is usually advisable if the plants have not branched by the time they are about 15cm (6in) high.

Begonias and gloxinias do not need stopping; but they must be potted on before they receive a check to growth, either into 7.5cm (3in) pots of potting compost from the boxes in which they were started, or into 12.5-15cm (5-6in) pots if they are already in small ones. Both plants need shade from full sun and gloxinias also prefer a humid atmosphere.

As soon as cyclamen seedlings are about 5cm (2in) high, with several leaves, pot them singly into 7.5cm

Perpetual flowering carnations need airy, rather dry conditions.

(3in) pots of potting compost with the top of the tiny corm just level with the surface. Subsequent waterings will then leave it at the right level, with its upper half exposed. Water the seedlings in after potting but then keep them warm and fairly dry until growth starts again.

If dahlia tubers have not already been started, box them up immediately to provide cuttings. Cuttings can be taken from tubers started earlier as soon as the new shoots are about 5cm (2in) high. Sever them close to the base and insert them in a warm, close frame.

Cuttings of the outdoor and greenhouse decorative chrysanthemum may also still be taken — the sooner the better — while those taken earlier must be potted up as they become rooted. Chrysanthemums for pot culture will be ready for their final potting early next month so make sure that pots, compost and crocks are all in hand.

In milder areas outdoor tomatoes should be sown now for June planting. Continue to prick out or pot up the earlier sown ones for greenhouse cultivation, then plant them out as soon as they are 15-23cm (6-9in) high in deeply dug, well-drained soil, with plenty of compost or old manure well down and a dressing of a tomato base fertilizer in the top spit. Or ring culture can be carried out by planting in an appropriate potting compost (mixture) in bottomless containers on a layer of gravel. Make sure that the plants are moist at the root before putting them in, then water them sparingly. Do not allow the 'soil ball' to become dry.

Although not ideal companions for tomatoes, one or two cucumbers will yield enough fruits for domestic use. Sow the seeds 12mm (½in) down in 8cm (3½in) pots of moist potting compost and keep them in a temperature of 21°C (70°F).

Insect pests, such as greenfly, mealy bug and red spider mite, will be rapidly on the increase now. So spray or fumigate at the first sign of them.

Opposite: using cloches it is possible to have early lettuces.

May

The greenhouse is likely to be bursting at the seams with young stock now, but the position can be eased by putting many of the summer bedding plants out into frames to be hardened off. This should be done by increasing the ventilation at first during day, then at night. Protect the plants from cold winds and, to avoid drying out, which will occur more readily in the frames than in the greenhouse, give them copious waterings in hot weather. Dahlias in pots may also be hardened off now.

Hot weather will also mean shading and if this can be done by an automatic arrangement so much the better — otherwise slatted blinds, a proprietary shading solution or a mixture of flour and water will have to be used. Increased damping down, by wetting the floor and stagings (benches) will also be needed to maintain a certain amount of humidity but the atmosphere must also be kept bouyant by generous ventilation.

Most of the main sowings have been made by now but three fine spring-flowering pot plants that should be sown between now and July are cinerarias, *Primula malacoides* and the greenhouse calceolarias. These are all colourful plants which hold their flowers for relatively long periods. They are well worth taking the trouble to raise.

Hydrangeas coming into bloom will need liberal watering and light shade, together with frequent feeding for all but blue varieties, which must not be given too much nitrogen or the colour will be poor. Cuttings of hydrangeas may also be taken now, using unflowered shoots taken off about 10cm (4in) long and inserted in a peat-sand moisture in a close frame.

As the earliest hippeastrums pass out of bloom cut out the flowered stem, then keep the plants well watered and fed in full light for the rest of the summer. Cyclamen that have died down should be kept perfectly dry in full sun, while arum lilies (*Zantedeschia aethiopica*) should always be given full light but gradually less water after flowering.

Schizanthus must be potted on before they become pot-bound. Move those in 7.5cm (3in) pots on into 15cm (6in) ones of an appropriate potting compost (mixture) and autumn-sown ones, already in 12.5-15cm (5-6in) pots, into 20 or 23cm (8 or 9in) ones.

By about the second week of May chrysanthemums for pot culture in the greenhouse will need their final potting into 23 or 25cm (9 or 10in) pots, according to the vigour of the variety. The quickest way to do this is to stand the pots out on the standing ground where the plants are to spend the summer, fill each one with an appropriate potting compost to about 5cm (2in) from the top and then set the plant in the compost so that the base of the stem is just level with the surface. The plants should, of course, be hardened off before potting them outside.

Tomatoes planted in the greenhouse will be making rapid growth now, but do not encourage them too much by watering and feeding or the bottom truss may not set. Aim at slow steady growth by adequate, but not excessive, watering and use a feed containing a high proportion of potash. Make sure that all sideshoots where the leaves join the stem are removed as soon as they can be handled without damage.

Cucumber seedlings in 8cm (3½in) pots must be kept warm and moist and in a humid atmosphere until they are about 15cm (6in) high, when they should be ready for planting out on the greenhouse bench 60cm (2ft) apart on mounds of rich humus soil with perfect drainage.

For greenhouse display, fuchsias and geraniums grown from cuttings will need moving on into 12.5cm (5in) pots of an appropriate potting compost or the trailing kinds can be used in hanging baskets together with *Campanula isophylla*, *Lobelia tenuior*, *Begonia pendula*, *Nepeta hederacea* (*glechoma*) and similar trailing plants. To keep the baskets moist without heavy watering, line them out with moss, then with polythene sheeting, before putting the plants in.

Keep climbing plants trained in and to ensure that the passion flower (*Passiflora caerulea*) flowers well it should be kept fairly dry with no feeding.

Strawberries are justly the most popular greenhouse fruit.

1. *Schizanthus, often called poor man's orchid, will have a mass of bloom if given a rich soil.*
2. *Bougainvillea is a strong climber with showy flower-like bracts, and does best in warm conditions.*

3. *Calceolaria is strictly a perennial but is treated as an annual to ensure really vigorous plants.*
4. *Gardenia jasminoides is one of the most powerfully scented of all shrubs suitable for the greenhouse.*

June

Dahlias, zonal pelargoniums ('geraniums'), fuchsias, zinnias, *Salvia splendens*, cannas, *Begonia semperflorens*, heliotropes and gazanias may all be planted out now from the cold-frames, if they have been well hardened off. If there are any surplus plants, some of them should be potted up into 12.5cm (5in) pots for summer flowering in the greenhouse but a few of the pelargoniums will also come in useful for winter flowering if all the flower buds are removed until the end of September.

The empty frames can then be used for those pot-plants coming on for next winter and spring, such as cyclamen, *Primula obconica*, *P. malacoides*, cinnerarias and calceolarias, as soon as these are in their final pots. Some of them will already be in 7.5-8cm (3-3½in) pots, but others will still be in the boxes in which they were pricked out. In the latter case the plants must be moved on into 7.5-8cm (3 ir 3½in) pots just before their leaves meet in the boxes, when each one should be potted singly in an appropriate potting compost (mixture).

Make sure their roots are moist before moving the plants on and see that they are potted moderately firmly with about 12mm (½in) left at the top of the pot for watering. Plants without an obvious stem must not be buried too deeply; just keep the plant level with the surface of the compost.

Plants already in small pots will be ready for their final potting as soon as the roots can be seen in the drainage holes.

After making certain that the plants are moist at the root, knock each one out of its pot and set it in a 12.5 or 15cm (5 or 6in) one, filled with an appropriate potting compost over good drainage so that when the potting is done there will be a space of about 18mm (¾in) at the top of the pot for watering. Keep the plants shaded and slightly on the dry side for a few days after potting, then transfer them to the cold-frame. Here they will grow better and need less water if they are 'plunged', or

Hydrangeas do well as potted plants and provide a long display of colour.

buried to the pot-rim, in a mixture of peat, sand and sieved soil; or peat and sand alone can be used. Do not overcrowd the plants as their leaves must never be allowed to touch. Give them plenty of ventilation and shade them from full sun.

Solanum capsicastrum, the Christmas cherry, is another plant that should be similarly potted and plunged, but add a pinch of Epsom salts (magnesium sulphate) to each pot of compost (soil mixture). Then, when the plants produce their small white flowers, keep them well syringed to ensure a good 'set' of berries.

If the late-flowering plants are in the frames, the greenhouse can be used for the summer-flowering ones, such as gloxinias and tuberous begonias. To produce large flowers start to feed these as the pots fill with roots, giving weak doses at frequent intervals rather than stronger ones at longer intervals, with the feed always being given when the soil is already moist. Keep these and other summer pot-plants shaded from full sun. 'Damp down' and ventilate the greenhouse on hot days.

Pot-grown chrysanthemums now outside must be securely staked against wind damage. Use 1.2-1.5m (4-5ft) canes according to the height of the variety, with one or three canes

to each pot. If one is used, stand it upright in the pot and secure it to a wire stretched between two firm end posts. If three are used, splay them outwards and fasten two to the supporting wire. Watering of these chrysanthemums will need very careful attention, with a sufficient amount being given at each watering to soak the soil right through.

Plants of *Azalea indica* kept from last winter would go outside now. Plunge them to the pot-rim in peat or in a lime-free soil and keep them well watered and syringed with lime-free water — rain water, if necessary.

Tomatoes will need more water as they grow. See that all side-shoots are regularly removed and spray the plants overhead daily to help the fruit to set.

Greenhouse cucumber plants must be stopped when they are about 1.2m (4ft) high or at the top of the supporting wires. Remove all flowers from the main stem and all male flowers (those without an embryo fruit). Then, as the fruits appear, stop all shoots two leaves beyond the fruit.

Opposite: dwarf beans are prolific and easy-to-grow vegetables.

Leaf cuttings provide a fascinating method of propagating certain pot-plants now, notably the popular gloxinias, varieties of *Begonia rex* and saintpaulias.

There are several effective ways of taking these cuttings; but for glox-inias and saintpaulias a simple way is to cut off mature, but not old, leaves, each with a good 2.5cm (1in) of the leaf-stalk. Insert these upright in a mixture of peat and sand so that the base of the leaf-blade is just buried. After insertion keep them moist in a warm, close propagating frame.

For *Begonia rex* the simplest way is to use similar leaves with the main veins cut through in several places on the underside of the leaf, which should then be laid on a peat-sand mixture so that the cuts are firmly in contact with it. In the warm humid atmosphere of a close propagating frame new plantlets will then form at the cuts.

The popular 'busy Lizzie' (*Impatiens holstii* and *I. sultanii*) is even easier to root now. Cut off unflow-ered shoots 7.5-10cm (3-4in) long and stand them in a jar of water in full sun. Saintpaulias too may be rooted in water, by using leaves as mention-ed above and merely standing them in the water.

For the propagation of ivies (*Hedera*), *Ficus elastica* (the rubber plant) rhoicissus and the beautiful climbing *Hoya carnosa* leaf-bud cuttings may be taken now. Cut 2.5cm (1in) pieces of the stem so that each piece contains a leaf at its centre. Inset the leaves upright in a peat-sand mixture and keep them moist in a close frame.

Tuberous begonias cannot be pro-pagated by leaves, but the side-shoots that spring from the junctions of the leaves and main stem can be used. Take these off, 7.5-10cm (3-4in) long, where they join the stem and leaf-stalk, so that each one has a solid wedge-shaped base. Insert them in a peat-and-sand mixture in a close frame.

Tuberous begonias will need stak-ing now, or as soon as the flower buds form. When the buds appear they will be in threes, with a small one on either side of the large main one. In order to ensure extra large blooms remove these smaller side ones.

Cyclamen kept from last year should be repotted now. Shake them out of the old soil, remove any with-ered roots and repot in well-drained pots of an appropriate potting com-post (mixture) with the top of the corm just level with the surface. Give a thorough watering, then stand the plants in cool shade, where they should be given frequent over-head syringeing.

Further sowings of cineraria, cal-ceolaria and *Primula malacoides* may be made now to provide a succession. Tuberous begonias and gloxinias may also be sown now to provide young plants for storing through the winter.

As hydrangeas pass out of bloom, cut the flowered stems back to 15cm (6in) long. Repot into a size larger pot, using an appropriate potting compost and stand the plants in full sun outside, where they must be kept quite moist.

As regal pelargoniums finish flowering cut them back hard and rest them by laying the pots containing them on their sides outside. They will need little or no water for the next few weeks; but do not let them dry out completely.

Chrysanthemums in pots will need feeding from early July onwards. Use a fertilizer with a fairly high nitrogen content. Either a liquid or a dry feed may be used, but always follow the manufacturer's instruc-tions.

Perpetual carnations need plenty of water and ventilation now, to-gether with damping down and over-head syringeing to prevent too arid an atmosphere. Feeding, preferably

Actinidia chinensis is a vigorous climber bearing gooseberry- flavoured fruit, sometimes known as kiwi fruit.

with a commercial carnation fertilizer, should be carried out regularly from now until the end of October.

As soon as tomato plants have set their fourth truss feed with a nitrogenous fertilizer, such as dried blood, to prevent the tops of plants bearing a weight of fruits 'running off' thin.

As cucumber roots appear on the surface of the soil top dress with a 2.5cm (1in) thick layer of well-rotted manure mixed with good loam. If manure is not available use garden compost with a little general fertilizer added. Shade the plants from hot sun and syringe regularly to keep down red spider mite.

The passion flower, Passiflora caerulea, *makes a showy climber.*

August

One of the most useful plants to sow now is the cyclamen, to provide plants for flowering in 12-15 months' time. The seed, which is large enough to handle individually, is best sown 2.5cm (1in) apart and about 6mm (¼in) deep in a seed-pan or tray filled evenly and firmly with one of the soil-less seed composts (mixture).

Following sowing, soak the compost from underneath until it is wet right through and then stand the pan or tray in a warm part of the greenhouse, where it should be covered with glass and paper. If the compost is kept quite moist germination should take place in 4-5 weeks.

Another invaluable plant that may also be propagated now, but this time by cuttings, is the zonal pelargonium (geranium). Use unflowered shoots that are half-ripe (those with a distinct reddish tinge) trimmed immediately beneath a joint to about 10cm (4in) long. The cuttings may then be inserted around the edge of a pot of sandy soil or, for large quantities, in a bed of similar soil made up in a cold frame; or more simply, they may be merely dibbled into a piece of light, sandy soil in a sunny place in the garden, where they should root well but rather more slowly. Whichever method is used

make sure that the base of each cutting is firmly in contact with the soil, 2.5-4cm (1-1½in) below the surface.

Other cuttings that may also be taken are those of heliotrope and fuchsia. For the former use unflowered shoots 5-7.5cm) (2.3in) long trimmed off beneath a joint, and insert them fairly close together in a seedbox filled with sandy soil, finally placing them in a close frame.

Fuchsia cuttings to produce bush plants are not normally taken in summer, but for 'standard' fuchsias they should be put in now, using unflowered shoots about 7.5cm (3in) long. These will soon root if inserted around the edge of a pot of light, well-drained soil kept just moist in light shade on the greenhouse bench.

Of the bulbous subjects for late winter and spring flowering one of the first that should be put in is the freesia, invaluable both for its beauty and fragrance. Use an appropriate potting compost (mixture) made quite firm over good drainage in 12.5-15cm (5-6in) pots. Each pot will take from 6 to 8 corms respectively. Set the corms with their tops about 2.5cm (1in) beneath the surface then make the compost just moist and stand the pots in a cold-frame where if shaded from the sun. they should

Leaves can be as colourful and varied as flowers.

need no further water until growth starts. If no frame is available they may be stood in the open and protected from the rain.

Lachenalias, another useful plant for spring flowering, may also be grown from corms in exactly the same way now.

Arum lilies (*Zantedeschia aethiopica*) may also be started into growth now, using either newly purchased 'crowns' or old plants, which should be repotted if they have been in their present pots for more than a year. Alternatively, these old plants may be divided. One young plant or division will go into a 15cm (6in) pot or three into a 20-23cm (8-9in) pot, in either case using an appropriate potting compost (mixture) over good drainage. After potting keep the plants in the open and water sparingly until growth starts.

Mid-season chrysanthemums growing in pots normally start to produce their flower buds during August and for large blooms the plants must be disbudded by removing all but the main central bud on each stem. Any sideshoots appearing where the leaves join the stem should also be removed, together with longer sideshoots and suckers appearing near the base of the plant. Continue to feed the plants and guard against insect pests by spraying with approved sprays.

As the flowers fade on the greenhouse climber *Hoya carnosa*, cut off the dead blooms, but leave the actual flower-stalks intact, as these should produce further blooms for your pleasure next year.

Feed pot-plants such as cinerarias, calceolarias and primulas for winter and spring flowering with a complete fertilizer about once a week as soon as their roots can be seen in the drainage holes. The later batches, now in 7.5 or 8 cm (3in or 3½) pots must be potted into 12.5 or 15cm (5 or 6in) pots before they become pot-bound.

Ventilate tomatoes freely from now on to guard against leaf-mould (*Cladosporium*) and make sure that the atmosphere is kept fairly dry.

Opposite: Fuchsia '*Dutch Mill*', *one of many attractive hybrids.*

September

Hyacinths and narcissi, including daffodils, make a valuable contribution to the greenhouse display at Christmas or soon afterwards, so, to ensure these early blooms, get the bulbs planted in pots or bowls as early in the month as possible. For Christmas hyacinths use 'prepared' bulbs, one to a 10cm (4in) or three to 15cm (6in) pot and plant them in appropriate potting compost (mixture) if they are to go into pots, or in bulb fibre if they are to be grown in undrained bowls. The 'noses' of the bulbs should finish just above the surface. After planting, soak the potted ones well, then bury them beneath about 10cm (4in) of sand or weathered ashes in the garden. Those bulbs planted in bowls, however, are better in a cool, dark and airy place under cover. The main thing then is to make sure that the compost (soil mixture) is kept quite moist.

Daffodils and other narcissi are similarly treated, except that they can be planted rather closer together. Small bulbous subjects such as snowdrops, crocuses and muscari (grape hyacinths) may also be potted up quite close together now and plunged beneath sand or weathered ashes outside.

Winter- and spring-flowering pot-plants now in frames must be brought into a slightly heated greenhouse before there is any risk of severe frost. But they should be quite safe in the frames until at least the end of the month if the frames can be covered with mats or sacking on cold nights. But do not bring in hydrangeas yet. These plants must be left outside until all their leaves have fallen.

Most plants will need rather less water now, particularly hippeastrums, which should be gradually dried off. Achimenes, too, should be similarly dried off after they have flowered. Cacti also need less water now but keep them in full sun to ripen their growths properly. Regal pelargoniums, on the other hand, will already have had their resting and ripening period so these can be started into growth again. Cut them back to about 20cm (8in) high if this has not already been done, then re-pot into an appropriate potting compost (mixture) using pots one size larger than the present ones. After potting keep the plants in the greenhouse where they should be frequently syringed but at the same time watered sparingly until growth starts.

Two useful plants to sow now are schizanthus and mignonette for early summer flowering under glass. The schizanthus is best sown in a pot or seed-pan to provide seedlings for pricking out and potting on later. Mignonette, however, is best grown in the pots in which it is to flower. For this plant a rich, well-limed and very firm soil gives the best results, with the seeds being sown very thinly just beneath the surface. When the seedlings are large enough to be handled safely thin them out to leave the strongest ones about 2.5cm (1in) apart.

Towards the end of the month a start will have to be made on bringing the pot-grown chrysanthemums into the greenhouse, so make sure that this is cleared out and cleaned in readiness for them. Make sure that the chrysanthemum pots are as clean as possible and the plants themselves free from pests before housing them just close enough together to prevent one plant from touching another.

As soon as frame space becomes available a start can be made on the propagation of bedding plants from cuttings. The main ones to be taken are of violas, pansies, bedding calceolarias, antirrhinums and penstemons. For violas and pansies use strong young shoots springing from the base of the plant trimmed off beneath a joint to about 5cm (2in) long, but for the others use unflowered sideshoots similarly trimmed. The cuttings of all these plants should then be firmly inserted about 7.5cm (3in) apart in a firm, level bed of good sandy soil in the frame, where after a good watering-in they should be kept close until new growth indicates that rooting has taken place.

Early roses for cutting greenhouse display may be obtained by growing the plants in pots with or without artificial heat, although in the latter case the flowers will obviously be later. Recommended varieties should be ordered immediately for potting up in October.

Dormant plants of the extremely beautiful but tender *Azalea indica* should also be ordered now for potting next month.

Chrysanthemums are grouped according to flower shape. C. 'Pretty Polly', a medium-flowered reflexed decorative. Opposite: initial thinning will help to produce heavy bunches of grapes.

October

It is no longer safe to have tender pot plants in frames, even with extra protection, so get them in as soon as possible. But first clean the pots and give the plants a thorough spraying against insect pests.

To keep these and other plants safe, heating will have to be used from now on. A temperature of 7°C (45°F) is adequate for such subjects as cinerarias, *Primula malacoides*, freesias and the greenhouse calceolarias. For cyclamen and *Primula obconica* a temperature of 13°C (55°F) is more suitable, although the plants will come along more slowly in cooler conditions.

Given the temperature mentioned (and maximum light for the cyclamen) these last two plants may be watered liberally but in a lower temperature the compost (soil mixture) should be allowed to become almost dry before soaking it thoroughly, preferably from underneath. Cinerarias, *Primula malacoides* and calceolarias should also be watered in this way. Although dryness is unlikely to harm them, unless carried to extremes, over-watering may kill them.

Cacti and most succulents need even less water — one soaking a month is more than adequate. Only enough heat to keep frost out is needed for them but the Christmas cactus (*Zygocactus truncatus*) does better in a temperature of about 16°C (60°F) with enough water to keep it evenly moist.

Where dormant plants of the tender *Azalea indica* have been ordered they should be delivered at any time now. If they are not already in pots make sure that the soil-ball on the roots is quite moist, then set each plant in a pot just large enough to take it, with a lime-free mixture such as 2 parts peat and 1 of sand being worked in firmly round the roots. Give a thorough watering with lime-free water (rainwater if necessary) then keep the plants in a temperature of about 10°C (50°F) and allow them to dry a little before giving more water.

Continue to pot up hyacinths, tulips and narcissi (including daffodils) and the smaller bulbs. Make sure that those in bowls under cover are kept adequately moist in a dark, airy place.

Some of the other bulbous subjects will be going to rest now. Gloxinias and tuberous begonias, for instance, should be allowed to die down gradually after flowering until the old stems and foliage can be easily removed. Begonia tubers should then be stored, quite dry, in a cool but frostproof place, while the gloxinias should be stored in a temperature of at least 10°C (50°F). Store the smaller tubers of achimenes in the same way as gloxinias. Hippeastrums should be left in their pots and kept perfectly dry in cool, airy conditions.

Some of the perennial bedding plants such as geraniums, fuchsias, heliotropes and gazanias will also need storing now. If they are left outside much longer they may be damaged by frost. The geraniums (zonal pelargoniums) may be placed close together in boxes of light soil. They should be kept almost dry in a frostproof place through the winter. Fuchsias may be similarly dealt with or potted singly, with just enough winter watering to keep them alive. Heliotropes are best potted and stored in a temperature of at least 10°C (50°F). Gazanias too, are best potted singly, but if kept almost dry these only need enough heat to keep frost away. Cuttings of all these plants will probably be well rooted by now and ready for boxing or potting for storage in the same way as the old plants.

Complete the housing of pot-grown chrysanthemums as soon as possible and make sure they have plenty of fresh air circulating around them, with just enough heat to keep frost away. Water thoroughly when the soil on the surface dries. Disbudding will still have to be carried out on the later varieties if large blooms are required, while feeding should be carried out until the blooms are almost ready for cutting.

Hybrid tea roses for pot culture are best potted this month. Set each one in a 17.5cm (7in) pot with good drainage beneath a compost of good soil with a little old manure and enough coarse sand to keep the mixture open. A little bonemeal added to this mixture will also help. After potting, water the plants in, then stand them in the open until early next year, when they may be brought in for gentle forcing.

Cuttings of violas, pansies, bedding calceolarias, antirrhinums and penstemons may still be taken, while those that have already rooted should be grown on in conditions as cool and airy as the weather will permit. From now on plants need all the light they can get so remove any shading and clean the glass. Keep the air in the greenhouse as dry as possible and do all watering in the morning so that the plants are fairly dry at night.

Below: the Christmas cactus, Zygocactus truncatus, *flowers in winter. Opposite:* Chrysanthemum '*Madelaine Queen*'.

November

Fog and damp are the main enemies of greenhouse plants this month and against the former all you can do is to keep the ventilators closed while the fog persists. When it goes, ventilate freely and give a little more heat to freshen and dry the air. Avoid splashing when watering and make sure that there is ample room for air to circulate freely around the plants. If botrytis (a grey woolly fungus) appears remove affected leaves or plants immediately and give more air, even it if means lowering the temperature a little.

Pot-grown hydrangeas should now be brought in if their leaves have fallen. Place them in a cool, airy part of the greenhouse and water them only when they become almost dry.

Dahlia roots from outside should also be brought in — after the foliage has been blackened by frost. After lifting and roughly drying the tubers, store them loose in a box where they will be safe from frost. Each one must be labelled.

Cyclamen from an August sowing will be ready for pricking out as soon

Coelogyne cristata is a popular and showy orchid flowering in winter.

as they have made two or three tiny leaves. Use an appropriate potting compost (mixture) made firm and level in a seed-box and set the tiny corms about 4cm (1½in) apart, with the top of the corm just level with the surface. Subsequent waterings will then bring it to the correct level, with the upper half of the corm showing. After pricking out keep the seedlings on the dry side in full light, preferably in a temperature of 16°C (60°F) to encourage quick rooting.

Some of the hardy bulbs planted in pots or bowls in September will be ready for bringing inside if they have made 5cm (2in) of growth together with plenty of roots either coming through the drainage holes in pots or pushing up round the sides of bowls. If they have reached this stage bring them into gentle heat and give them gradually more light. Small bulbs such as crocuses, scillas and snowdrops should not be brought in until the flower spikes are visible.

For a spring display in a cold greenhouse, polyanthuses, wall-flowers, astilbes, Solomon's seal (*Polygonatum multiflorum*), *Dicentra spectabilis* and *D. formosa* 'Bountiful' should all be lifted and potted in good, well-drained soil. After potting bury them to the pot-rim in the ground outside to become established in the pots, then bring them in early next year.

Where the climbing passion flower (*Passiflora caerulea*) is grown under glass its rampant growth may shade other plants too much. In this case it may be safely cut back to about 45cm (18in) and kept fairly dry through the winter. Schizanthus plants sown in September should now be strong young plants in 7.5cm (3in) pots. Keep them as cool and airy as possible, preferably on a shelf close to the glass, and water sparingly.

Pot lilies, as they become available, in well-drained pots half-filled with an open, porous soil with plenty of leaf-mould added, and lime where necessary. Then stand the pots in a cold frame until growth starts.

Opposite: some of the most attractive effects in the greenhouse can be achieved simply by grouping together plants with bold and colourful contrasting foliage.

December

If all has gone well there should now be a good show of cyclamen, *Primula obconica*, *Solanum capsicastrum* (the Christmas cherry), *Azalea indica* and the first of the potted bulbs, such as *Narcissus* 'Paper White' and 'Soleil d'Or' and the earliest 'prepared' hyacinths. All of these may be in bloom by Christmas (or in berry in the case of the *Solanum*) but the plants should not be over-crowded as this will only encourage pests and diseases. If possible, stand them on tiered shelving on the staging so that each one has ample room.

The beautiful foliage plant *Begonia rex* is another one that can add to the display, but this needs a temperature of at least 10°C (50°F) if it is to keep its leaves. At this time of year give *B. rex* the benefit of full light and keep the compost just moist.

As the mid-season chrysanthe-mums finish cut them down to about 20cm (8in) high, wash the soil off the roots and set the roots (stools) close together in boxes of a good compost. Then keep them cool and fairly dry until they are started into growth early next year. The December-flowering varieties can then be spaced out farther apart to ensure a good circulation of air around them.

Zonal pelargoniums (geraniums) and fuchsias now in store will need an occasional look-over to make sure that they are not too dry. They need very little water but should not be allowed to dry out completely. A thorough soaking about once a month should keep them safe.

Where perpetual carnations are being grown the first cuttings may be taken now. Established plants should be kept in an even temperature, with a minimum of 7°C (45°F) at night, by careful regulation of the heating and ventilators. The plants need little water now but make sure that, when watering is necessary, the compost is wet right through.

Climbing plants of all kinds should be trained as necessary and kept on the dry side. This is a good time, too, to erect any necessary supports for them, using wires, trellis or one of the various metal meshes that are available.

Roses that were flowered in pots under glass last year may be brought in now for harder forcing. Renew the top inch or two of compost in the pots, prune the roses in the usual way and bring them into an initial temperature of 7°C (45°F). Water moderately and increase the temperature as the plants grow. Plants potted last autumn should not be started off until early next year, with only very mild forcing for the first season.

It is of course too soon to make any sowings for next year yet but the necessary materials for sowing, pricking-out and potting should be got ready before the weather clamps down on operations of this sort. A good supply of loam should, for instance, be placed under cover so that it is dry enough for sieving and possibly sterilizing when it is needed and a supply of peat should be sieved ready for use.

Sand, too, is another medium needing to be kept dry, otherwise it may be frozen solid when you need it. Pots, boxes and so on should be thoroughly cleaned and dried.

Hard frost may also loosen the cuttings that have been inserted in frames for the winter, so if necessary, firm them back into the soil, at the same time removing any dead leaves, weeds and other debris. It will also help if the soil between the cuttings is lightly pricked over by running the point of a dibber between the plants.

Finally, if the greenhouse plants do happen to get frozen spray them with cold water as early as possible next morning. This may just save them by preventing the too rapid thaw that does most of the damage to foliage and flowers.

Modern strains of Cineraria hybrida grandiflora.

Opposite: Greenhouse azaleas, are often forced for winter flowering.

143

Glossary

Annual

An annual is a plant which completes its life cycle (germination, flowering, setting seeds) within one growing season and then dies. This does not necessarily mean within a calendar year; an annual can be sown in early autumn and will complete its life cycle the following summer. Nor does the cycle always last as long as one year; some annuals, mainly weeds, go through several life cycles in the course of a single year. Annuals are subdivided into three main groups; hardy annuals, half-hardy annuals and tender annuals. The classifications are rather vague but, basically, they refer to the plant's degree of resistance to frost and ability to grow outside unprotected.

Axil

In gardening, the term axil refers to the angle formed between the leafstem and the parent stem of a plant. Sometimes this angle contains a leaf bud or a flower bud, known as the axillary bud. For certain crops you may need to 'pinch out' some or all of these buds, or the resulting axillary shoots. This is important in crops such as tomatoes, where the axillary buds are pinched out to stop the production of extra foliage and encourage fruit formation.

Biennial

A biennial plant is one that takes two full growing seasons to complete its lifecycle of germination, flowering, setting seeds and dying. Many vegetables are biennials, but they are treated as annuals; that is, they are harvested in the first year before they have had time to flower and seed.

Blanching

Blanching is the process of excluding light from growing plants, to prevent the production of chlorophyll (the colouring matter in the green parts of plants). This is done to certain vegetables to make them white, tender and more delicate in flavour. Leeks and endive are both vegetables which are blanched. The usual method for stem vegetables is to wrap the plant in cardboard, plastic sheeting or newspaper then earth it up. For endive and similar low-growing plants, the best method is to cover each plant with a clay pot, stopping up the drainage hole with putty or Plasticine.

Blind

A plant is blind when it loses its growing point and ceases to develop, often as a result of damage or disease. This is something to look for in thinning out seedlings, it is common in the cabbage family if seedling are attacked by cabbage root fly larvae. The plants appear healthy at first sight, but examination will show that the growing point is gone. No treatment can restore growth to blind plants, so dig up and discard them.

Bleeding

A plant is bleeding when it looses sap from a cut. A bit of bleeding is likely from any cutting, but it is most prevalent in the spring when the sap is rising. For this reason, stone fruit and vines should never be pruned in the spring, as they tend to bleed more than other plants. Bleeding is not harmful and treatment is not required, as healing is usually rapid. Some gardeners prefer to stop flows of sap by searing the cuts with a hot iron, or by painting with a commercial mixture. Beetroot (beets) will usually bleed if the skin or flesh is damaged, causing a loss of colour. To prevent this, be careful not to damage the skins when lifting the beetroot, and twist off the tops rather than cutting them.

Bolting
Plants which bolt are those which 'run to seed', meaning that they flower and produce seed too early. Bolting can be an inherited tendency, and breeders work hard to produce strains which will not bolt. Sometimes weather conditions will produce bolting, particularly in hot, dry summers. A check in growth will also occasionally produce bolting.

Bonemeal
Bonemeal is an organic fertilizer rich in phosphorous and calcium, and containing smaller quantities of nitrogen. It is made from the finely-powdered bones of animals, and it is useful when applied to acid soils. Bonemeal is a safe fertilizer which can be applied to all kinds of food crops.

Bordeaux mixture
One of the most valuable fungicides, Bordeaux mixture takes its name from the vineyards of Bordeaux where it was developed as a remedy for downy mildew. It is an extremely effective fungicide against such serious fungus diseases as potato blight, tomato blight and scab diseases of apples and pears.

Broadcast sowing
This is a method of sowing whereby seed is spread evenly over an area of ground, rather than placed in drills. Broadcast seed may be covered either by scattering soil over it or raking the surface carefully after sowing.

Bud
A bud is an embryo shoot or flower. Buds vary greatly in shape and character, and it is important for the fruit grower to be able to recognize the different types. A knowledge of buds is particularly useful in checking the progress of growth, recognizing if pruning is necessary and when this should be done. The two types that need to be carefully distinguished are the growth or shoot buds, and the blossom buds, which are often referred to as fruit buds. The growth buds are comparatively small and lie closer to the stem than the fruit buds. The fruit buds are larger and more prominent.

Bulb and bulbil
A bulb is a swollen underground bud surrounded by plump scales; these are, in fact, enlarged leaf bases. This bud is attached to a short stem and has roots which die annually. Some bulbs have a surrounding skin of dry papery scales. The bulb acts as a protector for the immature leaves and flowers found in the centre. An onion is a good example of a true bulb.

Callus
This is a growth of new tissue which forms naturally over a wound on a plant, particularly one made by pruning.

Captan
A widely used fungicide, captan is particularly effective against scab disease of apples and pears and against grey mould on strawberries. Captan is available both in liquid form for spraying and in powder form for dusting. Although not poisonous to humans, it is highly poisonous to fish and should not be used near a fishpond.

Catch crop
This is a quick-maturing crop which is put into the ground after one crop has been lifted but before the next crop in the rotation plan is planted.

Composts (Garden)

Not to be confused with seed or potting composts, garden compost consists of various organic matter allowed to rot down in a compost heap or bin, for use as a substitute for animal manure or as an addition to it. Like manure, it improves and enriches the soil by adding humus and plant nutrients. There are various different systems for making compost; all of them need air, moisture and nitrogen. The compost heap should be constructed so that air can penetrate it, it should be regularly moistened, and small amounts of a nitrogen-containing activator, usually manure or a nitrogenous fertilizer, should be added.

Compost (seeds and potting)

The word 'compost' is also used to refer to the loam- or peat-based mixtures that are used for raising seedlings (seed composts) or for growing plants in pots (potting composts). The best-known loam-based composts are the John Innes Composts, made to a standard formula developed at the John Innes Horticultural Institution. Reliable loamless (peat-based) composts are the University of California composts. Potting composts contain plant food to nourish the growing seedlings or pot-plants.

Cordon

Cordons are plants which have been pruned and pinched out so that they are restricted to a single main stem, or sometimes to two or three main stems. Fruit trees and bushes are often grown as cordons against fences or walls. A single (oblique) cordon is usually planted at an angle of 45°. Double and triple cordons are usually trained vertically, although a double cordon may be trained horizontally. Cordons take up little room — for example, cordon apples or pears can be planted as close as 60cm (2ft) apart — but the trees should be grown on dwarfing rootstocks, otherwise it is difficult to keep them growing as cordons without the fruitfulness disappearing.

Corm

A corm is a food storage organ which is a swollen underground stem, lasting a year. A new corm then forms to replace the old.

Cross-pollination

The transfer of pollen from one flower to another, usually between plants of the same species, is known as cross-pollination. The male pollen unites with (fertilizes) the female ovules in the flower to form a seed. Self-pollination occurs when the pollen is transferred from the male parts of a flower to the ovules of the same flower. Cross-pollination generally produces more vigorous plants and enables new characteristics to appear, and self-pollination is often actually prevented by the structure of the flower. Cross-pollination is of importance to the gardener in that plant breeders use it to combine the characteristics of two different varieties of a plant to produce a new, improved variety. It is also important in fruit growing; some fruit, such as sweet cherries, blueberries, and some apple, pear and plum varieties, are self-fertile — they crop only poorly or not at all when fertilized with their own pollen, but crop well when cross-pollinated by certain varieties of the same kind of fruit.

Cutting

A piece of plant taken from stem, leaf, bud or root, planted so that it will put out roots and grow into a new plant. It is one method of vegetative propagation.

Damping down

This is the operation of soaking the stagings (benches) and paths in a greenhouse with water, to create and maintain a high air humidity.

Derris

A vegetable-based insecticide effective against raspberry beetles, caterpillars, wasps and red spider mites. Is poisonous to fish so must be kept away from pools.

Dibber (dibble)

This is a tool used for making holes in the soil in which to sow seeds or plant seedlings or cuttings. The size of the dibber to be used depends on the size of the seeds or plants. Large dibbers are manufactured with wooden handles and steel tips, which can be pushed into the soil easily, while others are made entirely of steel. You can easily make your own dibber from an old spade or fork handle. For very small seeds or plants, a pencil or piece of dowelling can be used. A dibber should have a round, not a pointed, tip. If a pointed dibber is used, an air space will be left beneath the plant and the roots will be unable to take in food and water. The planting of a large number of young plants can be done much more quickly with a dibber than with a trowel.

Disbudding

This term usually refers to the removal of buds of such plants as roses, carnations, dahlias and chrysanthemums so that they produce a few flowers of exhibition size, but it is also used to describe the removal of buds on the young shoots of fruit trees, to help shape the trees or increase the crop of fruit.

Division

This is a method of vegetative (i.e. non-sexual) propagation, in which a plant is separated into two or more parts, each part complete with roots and growth buds.

Drill

Shallow furrow made in the soil in which seeds are sown.

Grafting

To grow one type of plant on the root or base stem of another plant. The lower stem and roots are called the rootstock, and the plant grafted on to the roots is called the scion.

Harden off

Gradually accustoming plants raised in protected conditions to outside temperatures and ventilation. If the process is too hurried, growth is checked and leaves can show signs of bad health.

Lateral

A side growth, either a branch or a shoot. When pruning, make sure you distinguish between laterals and leading or terminal shoots, often known as the leader which is at the end of the branch. Laterals are usually cut back harder than leaders.

Layering

Pegging a long healthy shoot to the ground after making a short cut through joint (or node), so that plant will root from this area into earth. Air layering means that damp sphagnum moss is wrapped around a cut branch if it cannot be bent down to the ground.

Malathion

An organophosphorus insecticide useful in the control of aphids, scale insects, thrips, beetles and fruit tree red spider mites. Sweet peas, ferns and zinnias are plants that can be damaged by use of the spray. Of short persistence.

Mulch
Insulating layer of various materials put over soil to prevent loss of water by evaporation. Some mulches also feed the soil slowly.

Nicotine
A vegetable-based poison useful as an insecticide against aphids, capsids, sawflies and leafminers. It is extremely poisonous to humans when in the concentrated state. Mark POISON; store under lock and key and never decant into harmless-looking containers. Of short persistence.

Node
Point in stem from which a leaf grows.

Organic
Derived from decaying natural (i.e. once-living) substances.

Prick out
To lever seedlings out of their seed box as soon as they can be handled and to transplant into deeper seed boxes with slightly richer soil.

Pyrethrum
Flower heads of species of *Pyrethrum* (now botanically classified under Chrysanthemums) produce this insecticide, which has a paralysing effect on insects. Decomposes rapidly, particularly in bright sunshine. Sometimes combined with other insecticides in commercial products. Useful and safe when combined with derris to produce an insecticide of short persistence.

Rhizome
Underground stem or creeping rootstock usually growing horizontally from which shoots or flowers come.

Rootstock
Word with two meanings, either used as with the above term, or used to described (more frequently) the root system on which a cultivated variety of plant has been budded or grafted.

Strike
To strike a cutting is to get the cutting to form roots and grow.

Terminal
At the end of branch or leaf.

Tuber
Enlarged part of a root or underground stem lasting a year only.

Variety
Plant varying from typical form of a species, in colour, shape or habit. Used commonly about any plant differing from the typical form.

Index

Numbers in *italics* refer to illustrations.